Women have the stren
obstacle that comes th
insightful wisdom and e
women who have encountered some of life's biggest
challenges. Be prepared to leap out of your comfort
zone and straight into your purpose.

Are you ready to break through your fears, overcome
your obstacles and embrace your true purpose? The
empowering stories included in this book will help you to
step into your purpose and finally share your special gifts
with the world.

*   *   *   *

When women embrace their purpose they can truly impact
the world. Alone each story is powerful but together they
will EMPOWER YOU to relish every breakthrough, every
discovery and every triumph of your life!

- **Kendall SummerHawk**, Leading Expert on Women
Entrepreneurs and Money
KendallSummerHawk.com

I can almost guarantee that you will see yourself in one
of the stories shared by these remarkable women; that
you will be touched by what they share of their own
journey; and that you will be inspired to think more deeply
about your life, why you are here, and what you are
meant to do.

- **Terri Zwierzynski**, President of Solo-E.com and
Advocate for the Solo Entrepreneur Lifestyle

EMPOWER is an international soup of inspired stories
flavored by women of all persuasions who have been
there and lived to tell about it.

- **Gina Mazza**, Author, Global Journalist,
and Creative Muse

EMPOWER!

Women's Stories of Breakthrough,
Discovery and Triumph

Dedication

To any woman who has a dream in her heart.

To Dawne & Mark

Thank you for your
friendship and love.
God bless,
love,
Cindy

To Dawne & Mark
Thank you for your
friendship and love.
God bless.
[signature]

Contents

Contents

Contents

Dr. Jan Cincotta

"Inside you there's an artist you don't know about. Say yes quickly, if you know, if you've known it from before the beginning of the universe."

- Jalai ud-Din Rumi

Chapter One:

BEGIN AGAIN

*W*hen people ask me what I do for a living, I never know how to answer. I tell them I'm a physician and a writer, although I don't currently earn a living as either one. I retired a couple of years ago and even though nothing I've written since then has earned a penny, I don't regret my decision at all.

I closed my practice after 30 years as a family physician for one reason: I wanted to write. I have always wanted to write. This, I learned, is not uncommon among doctors. Anton Chekhov, Sir Arthur Conan Doyle, John Keats and Oliver Wendell Holmes were all physicians who became successful authors. On a more contemporary note, Michael Palmer, Tess Gerritsen, Michael Crichton, Robin Cook and CJ Lyons come to mind.

The question is: How can a physician like myself claim to practice medicine, nurture a marriage, tend to the children, maintain a happy home, and still find time to write? How can anyone? The answer is (check all that apply):

We are blessed with a spouse who loves nothing more than to be left alone to do the nurturing, tending and maintaining without us.

We are geniuses who scoff at the mere thought of sleep.

We are delusional or on drugs.

I am half-joking about that third one but the fact is that most of us have trouble juggling all the roles we take on. The nature of a doctor's work requires us to set priorities yet they can change in a heartbeat . . . literally. Life and death situations take precedence over the needs of our own children. Their care may fall to someone else at a moment's notice. The marriage is expected to survive on its own. And when the housework clamors for attention, you sometimes have to tell it to pipe down, for crying out loud, you'll get to it. There is only so much a woman can accomplish in a day unless she thrives on exhaustion. Some women may be able to make this work but for me, it makes no sense whatsoever. So, I guess the answer for most physician-authors is that we abandon the practice of medicine because we are compelled to write.

When I left, I was old enough to convince my colleagues and patients that I was retiring, not quitting. It wasn't as though I simply got fed up with the job, turned in my stethoscope and slammed the door on my way out of the office. I agonized over the decision for three years before I finally summoned the nerve to let go of everything in life that was familiar and secure in order to begin all over again.

I didn't leave because of the long hours, or the fact that I'd been running hopelessly behind schedule all day, every day for three decades. I didn't leave to take an

easier position or to make more money. I didn't ask to be excused because of fatigue or forgetfulness or ill health. It's just that I felt so old, as though time was running out for me and there was so much I still wanted to do. The adage, "Life is too short," takes on new meaning as we age. It's too short to stifle desire, dwell in regret or abandon hope. Time passes too quickly to neglect longing, withhold passion or delay gratification. Sooner or later, you have to act on your own behalf.

As women, we tend to devote ourselves freely and generously to the hopes, expectations and needs of the people around us, while we scoot our own needs away with a flick of the wrist. "Get lost," we say. And they do.

Perhaps, like me, you ache to change careers, or to try something new. Photography. Meditation. Tap dancing. But you put it off because something always gets in the way. Maybe you have an unpublished poem collecting dust in a drawer somewhere. Every so often, you pull it out and revise a couple of lines, but invariably you put it aside again when something more pressing comes up. Perhaps there's an unfinished canvas moldering in your closet because your paints have dried up. Maybe you'd like to take a class or join the choir, but you don't have the time or energy because you work all day. And your family needs you. The dust bunnies have morphed into gorillas, your partner is lonely and the kids have had it with leftovers. The truth is that dirty dishes and laundry can wait; dreams cannot. Anyone can haul the garbage out but not everyone can write a poem or paint a rainbow. I've learned that dust gorillas are exceptionally tame and they love it when you read to them. And, properly refrigerated, food stays fresh for days.

So, if snatches of dialogue come to you in the middle of

the night, you doodle just for the fun of it, or you like to dance when no one is watching, it may be time to surrender to your muse. Until you begin, you will never know what you can accomplish. If you don't put your passion to the test, exercise your creativity and take steps to realize your dreams, you will never know if you have what it takes, and you will always wonder about it.

For me, the urge to write festered out of sight like an untended wound, aching and throbbing until I could no longer ignore it. Gradually, an unfulfilled hunger grew into longing, and longing hardened into stubborn resolve.

An opening line would come to me when I was driving to work, a character would speak up while I was reading an EKG, or a scene would unfold just as I drifted off to sleep. I recorded substantial portions of my manuscript on napkins, on the back of receipts and prescription blanks, and, if necessary, on the back of my hand, long before I actually sat down to write. Three years later, I finished my first novel and started the second one. I published a short story. Every week I post a literary blog online. Every day, I write.

When I started medical school, I had realistic expectations for my future. When I started this second career, I didn't know what to expect. I didn't have a master's in fine arts, nor do I have one now. I had no acquired expertise and no prior experience. I didn't know how to get started nor do I know how it will end. Will I ever publish that novel? Is it worth the effort? What will people think if I fail?

The point is that if you have a dream and the irresistible urge to actualize it, you may struggle with self-doubt,

4

too. Whenever we climb out of a comfortable rut and take off on an unfamiliar path, uncertainty lurks around every bend, especially when we choose to follow something as fleeting as a creative urge or as capricious as a dream.

> *" Excuse yourself and hurry to someone who encourages you and supports your dream. "*

As if your own misgivings weren't bad enough, you may hear voices. It may be the voice of a parent or partner imploring you to get serious, or ranting at you about earning a decent living or planning a secure future. It may be the voice of a teacher or boss or co-worker, all of them claiming to have "your best interests at heart" as they scatter disparagement along the path (as if your journey weren't difficult enough without them).

Worse is that it may be your own discouraging voice that you hear. You tell yourself that you'll never find success, that you're foolish or selfish or conceited for frittering away time when you're capable of so much more. Feeding the poor. Sheltering the homeless. Or in my case, healing the sick. Your own voice can make you feel guilty for indulging in something that is enjoyable and fulfilling when everyone else is hard at work. Exhausted. Empty. You feel unworthy if someone encourages or congratulates you. And should you experience a moment of inspiration, a surge of confidence or a glimmer of optimism, you convince yourself not to fall for it. Not to trust it. It doesn't mean a thing.

If you hope to follow your dream, you need to brace

yourself against these voices of restraint, shame and guilt. If people question your sanity, roll your eyes, sigh poignantly and shrug your shoulders at them. If they insinuate that you could put your time to better use, gaze heavenward and plead for divine intervention on their behalf. If that doesn't work, you must politely excuse yourself and hurry to your nearest friend... someone who encourages you and supports your dream. Someone who understands how hard this is and respects you for trying. Someone whose friendship isn't invested in your success or wealth or fame. Whatever you do, don't alter a word of your story, a stroke of your brush or a step of your dance in deference to the critics who (whether they admit it or not) envy you for doing what they may not have the courage to do themselves.

When you begin, remember that as a child, your first step, your first meaningful word, your first recognizable doodle all required untiring practice and monumental patience until BAM! Success! This will, too. Contrary to the few naysayers, no one expects you to run a marathon or paint a masterpiece or sing an aria in the beginning. Nor should you compare yourself with the master whose work you so admire. Do not be discouraged because others have already discovered their voice, taken to the stage, or published a book. Their success is proof that you can do it, too.

When you write or draw, keep an eraser and plenty of clean, white paper close at hand. If you are learning to dance, expect to stumble. When you sing, try for the high notes, too. Your first faltering efforts encourage the rest of us; and for a beginner, encouragement is right up there with wishful thinking, blind faith and cherished illusions.

I invested three years in my novel. I wrote the first draft in

longhand, the hardest thing I've ever done. It underwent countless revisions. I queried 50 literary agents about it, to no avail. Still, it is my proudest accomplishment.

So, please raise your hand if you are ready to begin. Raise your hand if today is the day. Don't wait, like I did, until you're old enough to retire. Begin with a visit to the art store. Sign up for that class. Get out your notebook. Forget for a moment the safe, secure grind you've been trained to believe in.

Trust your soul on this one.

Dr. Janet Cincotta acquired a passion for deep snow as a child growing up in western New York. She earned a bachelor of science degree in medical technology from the University of Vermont and her M.D. at SUNY Upstate Medical Center in Syracuse. A family physician for more than 30 years, she is presently at work on her second novel, as well as a memoir. She posts a weekly literary blog at www.ABeginnerAgain.blogspot.com. She and her husband occupy an empty nest in south central Pennsylvania.

Kelly Eckert

"Within us there is someone who knows everything, wills everything, does everything better than we ourselves."
\- Hermann Hesse

Chapter Two

WRITE YOUR OWN TICKET

I was in the car with my 14- and 12-year-old daughters and my two-year-old son when I got the phone call from my sister: "Dad's dead. He shot himself." Like an amazing act of divine symbolism, our phones cut out. It was a message I didn't want to hear, a message I didn't think I was ready to hear. But as I sat there silently clutching the steering wheel, reality seeped in. My father had killed himself. Whatever he had been suffering from, he was finally free. The deeper message took longer for me to hear: I was the one who was finally free.

From the time I was in third grade and an IQ test told my dad how smart I was (since I guess he couldn't figure it out on his own), he pushed me to go to Harvard. "With a Harvard degree, you can write your own ticket," he promised me. In my child's mind, I always wondered, *A ticket to where?* I had this image of picking a destination, a job or a dream and magically it would be so; the world would literally be my oyster. I only had to choose what I wanted.

There was one little glitch, though. What I wanted to

choose for myself was quite different from what my dad wanted me to choose. Even back then, I sensed that Dad was living vicariously through me. He would often mention how he regretted not doing well in school, not going to a better college, not becoming a lawyer. He would speak passionately about the law, and being highly empathic, it was easy for me to get swept up in his excitement. My father said that he wanted something better for me, and his "plan" was to see me become a lawyer then a judge. "Don't waste your gifts, your intelligence, your ambition," he would advise, yet in the back of my mind, I knew that he wanted me to take the exact step-by-step path that he didn't take so he could bask in the glow of my "success."

For this reason, I grew up in what felt like a prison of my own making. For most of my childhood, I mistook my father's passion for my path, and I saw no way out of it. In high school, I went through an angst-filled, creative teenager phase in which I fantasized about becoming a poet. Writing poetry was my act of rebellion. One day, I decided to submit a particularly raw and indicting poem for publication in my school's literary magazine. In it, I told the world - at least the world of my schoolmates and teachers - that my good girl, straight A, fluent in French, honor council president, academic superstar exterior belied an inner essence and a secret yearning. In those stanzas, I "outed" my father as a man who seemed to love me only for bragging rights - about my grades, academic awards and athletic achievements. When the poem was published, my classmates and teachers lauded me for my honesty and courage.

"Oh my God, what is your dad going to say?" my friends asked, and I caved into the pressure of keeping silent about my soul-baring work of art.

The school didn't want to anger my dad so they did not send my family a copy of the magazine. Later, I showed the poem to my mother; her response was to reprimand and shame me for doing something that would hurt my dad's feelings. My feelings? They didn't seem to matter.

My whole purpose in writing and publishing this poem wasn't to blame or upset anyone. It was to free myself from my father's expectations and "dis-appoint" him as my judge. (It's sort of funny that he had always wanted to be a judge and I gave him that power over me.) Ultimately, I disappointed myself because I never showed him the poem. I had taken a tentative step into authenticity and vulnerability, only to withdraw into my fear of criticism and rejection. I guess I was not so honest and courageous after all.

I did end up going to Harvard for a bachelor of arts cum laude in biological anthropology. I'll never forget walking across the dais with my fresh diploma and being greeted by the beaming smile on my dad's face. Part of me felt incredibly lucky to have this champion cheering me on. I realized that all he ever wanted was the best for me but a part of me still saw his smile as a trophy for him. I still saw his hopes and dreams for me as an obstacle course I had to complete in order to win his love and approval. So far, in his eyes, I was "winning."

But winning my father's love this way meant that I was losing myself, and I knew it. I took baby steps onto a path of my own, but I was still afraid to leap. One small step was to get my teacher certification in high school biology. Becoming a teacher was most definitely not in my father's plans for me, but I did my teacher training at the Harvard Graduate School of Education, so that sort of made it all right.

Instead of going straight into teaching, I got a master of science in biology from Tufts Graduate School of Arts and Sciences - another baby step. Tufts isn't an Ivy League school but a master's degree in biology was impressive enough by Dad's standards. By this point, he knew I was not going to become a lawyer. I had decided against it after spending a torturous summer interning at a law firm. No offense to people who love the law; I was just happy to find out early on that it really wasn't for me.

Another small step away from my father's expectations included getting married right out of Harvard. The expectation had always been that I would get an advanced degree, get a job, get promoted to CEO then maybe get married, if I felt like it, when I was in my late thirties. My husband was also a Harvard graduate but he went into the Marine Corps after college; this was so far outside of "the plan" that it was virtually inconceivable to my dad.

In some ways, getting married right out of college was quite a leap for me, as well. To buck "the plan" even more, we had children almost immediately: our first daughter when I was 25 and our second when I was not quite 27. My life looked nothing like my father or I thought it would. In this, I had certainly succeeded.

For me, rebellion meant getting married, having kids and putting my career on hold. In some ways, making these choices felt empowering. But, as before, my rebellion was incomplete. I was still afraid of losing my father's approval and love, so I replaced one set of expectations with another.

When my daughters were two and four, I decided that I had been a stay-at-home mom long enough and was

ready to "to do something for myself." A cloudy vision was forming about what that might be, something about writing and inspiring people. And I started to feel excited. Something was actually feeling right.

But "writing and inspiring" isn't a real career - as I was told - so when it was suggested that I get an MBA, I dutifully applied and got into the business school at Rice University. I value my time at Rice, the people I met and the skills I learned. But my soul was sick and tired of being led astray, and it let me know in quite certain terms. In fact, the farther along this road I traveled, the more lost I became. And the more I denied what I really wanted in life, the sicker I became. I had started to get daily headaches in high school. My first bout of depression happened in 11th grade. Shortly after graduating from college, I was getting weekly migraines. By the end of the first year in business school, I felt as if I were physically falling apart. My migraines were now lasting several days every week. I was restless, anxious and couldn't sleep. I had a serious bout of depression and was diagnosed with a seizure disorder.

I realized that when we don't listen to the whispers of our soul, it will hit us over the head with a sledgehammer to get our attention.

After a few hits from this spiritual sledgehammer, I finally listened. I heard my soul screaming, "Stop living a life that doesn't belong to you! Live the life that YOU had intended for yourself. Find your true path and follow it."

My first real moment of empowerment came when I handed in my letter of resignation at Rice University. In spite of the migraines and burgeoning depression, I had completed the first year with flying colors, done a summer internship, and was just starting the second and final year of the program. I was nine months away from having my MBA. And I quit. I dropped out.

That is when MY life truly began.

How to proceed onto the path of my "own" life didn't become clear right away; far from it. After leaving business school, I also ended my wobbly marriage. I worked as a professional artist for five years then reinvented my career and became a marketing consultant, freelance editor and graphic designer. I moved from Mexico to Houston to Pittsburgh. I got remarried and had a third child, a son. Over the course of a decade, I zig-zagged along the on-ramp to my True Path. I knew I was close because everything I was doing at the moment felt more right than anything I had done before. But something was still missing; I didn't feel completely whole or integrated. I needed for all that I had accomplished to fully come together.

That's when my father committed suicide.

During that decade leading up to his death, I watched helplessly from the sidelines as my father attempted suicide twice before he finally took his own life in October 2008. He had distanced himself from my sister and me, and the little girl inside me took it to mean that he didn't love me; after all, I wasn't living up to his expectations.

After he died and I realized that his death had freed me from his expectations, I had a deeper epiphany, one that planted me firmly and for good on my True Path and formed the very foundation of my new career. What I realized and what my father never did realize is that we all have the ability to write our own ticket every day with every decision we make. A Harvard degree is not required, nor is any degree. The simple act of choosing is all you need.

My father had been unhappy in his life, but he never accepted that he had a choice. He lived with his regrets instead of making choices that could have changed his course. Nothing was stopping him from going to law school later in life - except his own limiting expectations and his own fear. He had given up his dream of becoming a lawyer because he was following the path expected of him by his parents, and it made him miserable. He wanted something different for me, and yet we had both fallen into the same pattern of creating and meeting expectations. Fear can be fatal, and following any path other than your own can be soul crushing and literally life ending.

That message really hit home, and that's when I decided to become a life coach. I knew about coaching from a friend who was a certified life coach, but the idea didn't hit me right away. I spent that first year after my father's death grappling with survivor's guilt and how to live in a way that would honor both me and my father. I considered sticking with marketing consulting or editing, but I knew I wanted to do more than help people express themselves in the world. I wanted to help them figure out who they are at their core. You see, I realized that what I had been doing - in my art, as a marketing consultant, as an editor and graphic designer, and as a mom and wife - was helping other people to fulfill their goals, to find their way on their chosen paths. I wanted to help them not only take steps on their path, but also find their True Path.

It dawned on me that I am the spotlight that helps other people find their way. Finally, I felt whole. Everything made sense. I felt empowered to fulfill my purpose in a very straightforward way. And so I am. As a coach, I help others release their fears and transform limiting expectations so they can find and follow their true path.

> " *Our lives are filled with little moments of empowerment.* "

I have witnessed the tragic consequences of not being true to oneself and I wanted to choose differently. Some 30 years after first reading Robert Frost's poem "The Road Less Travelled," I finally understood its deep meaning. The road less travelled is not the path that fewer people follow but the one unique path that belongs to only you. It is called that because so few people choose to follow their own path. At the risk of sounding cliché, following my True Path has made all the difference in terms of my fulfillment, peace, happiness and contributions. It has transformed my relationships, my level of compassion and empathy, and even my ability to make better business decisions.

Our lives are filled with little moments of empowerment. The trick is to notice them, recognize them for what they are, and leverage them for full effect. Too often, women dismiss or diminish these moments. How many times have you said, "Oh, it's nothing," or "Anyone could have done it," or "It sure took me long enough"? Every empowered step we take creates ripples - or full-blown waves - that we can ride to greater empowerment... or not. Too often we choose to stop because the next step feels too risky or we're afraid of what might happen if we "rock the boat." I'm here to tell you that you can't worry about rocking someone else's boat. They are in charge of their own boat; you are only in charge of yours.

The heart-breaking yet valuable lesson that I've learned is that, in the end, I couldn't save my father; I could only save myself. Now, my life's work is about helping others save themselves. In this way, I am as much of a poet as any other; I help others get to the core of their truth, no matter how gut wrenching or wonderful it is. In living our truth, we become truly free.

Kelly Eckert, *MS, CMC, ACC, is a holistic life coach, speaker and author who works with visionaries, leaders, performers and artists to reach their highest potential and bring their deepest vision to life without losing themselves or selling their souls.*

Kelly is the creator of the Fear Releasing Method™ and the originator of Ayuratha energy healing and alignment. She has degrees in biological anthropology from Harvard and biology from Tufts. She received a teacher certification from the Harvard Graduate School of Education and studied marketing and entrepreneurship at the Rice University Jones Graduate School of Business.

Her other books are: Make Someone's Moment *and* Getting What You Want: How to Go from Stuck to Success. *Learn more at* <u>www.KellyEckert.com</u>.

DeLores Pressley

"The way you treat yourself teaches others how to treat you. Review your self-treatment plan often."
- DeLores Pressley

Chapter Three

YOU ARE GOOD ENOUGH!

*A*s I write this, I think of how I found my courage and became a confident person. Having lost my mother in recent years, I cannot help but reflect on my childhood and how she taught me to stand tall. As a young girl, I was always bigger and taller than everyone in my class, including the boys. I would scrunch my shoulders so that I could appear shorter. "Don't do that," my mother would say. "Stand tall. You are a beautiful girl." She called me her precious queen. How blessed I've been to have a mother who gave me such sustainable confidence. She set the tone for my life at a very early age.

Whenever I had a challenge, she would always find good in it. As a child, I was relentlessly teased by my peers (and many adults) about being tall and big. In my second book, *Clean Out the Closets of Your Life,* I shared how I wanted to be a ballerina but the dance instructor would not permit me to take ballet because I was too fat; instead, I was signed up for tap class because they said it would help me lose weight. I wanted to be a ballerina more than anything in the world. My best friend and I would dance around the house and talk about being dancers. My reed-thin friend had the opportunity to take ballet lessons. Because of the values my mother instilled in me, I was able to overcome the negative thoughts that went through my mind when I was told "no" to becoming a ballerina. But in the back of my mind, I felt the instructor was basically saying, "DeLores is not good enough."

During my junior year at Timken Vocational High School, I told my school counselor that I wanted to go to college. She clearly reminded me that it was a vocational school and I should learn a trade and forget about college. "You are not here for college. No, you are not going to college." I thought, Here we go again. I am not good enough. I was devastated but that "no" was my avenue for growth.

> *" Mom always found good in any challenge I encountered. "*

I did eventually go to college and received a bachelor of science degree in education. While I went on to teach elementary school for 27 years, I always owned a business during those years. I loved teaching but I simply wanted to teach and reach a larger audience at the same time. So I decided to try my luck at modeling. This led to more "no's", as I was repeatedly rejected by modeling agencies. Modern society had not yet recognized plus-size women as models, so no professional agency would take me seriously.

This "you are not good enough" theme continued in my

life, but so had the confidence that my mother instilled in me. So with that, I decided to create my own opportunities by starting a modeling agency. Many people around me had the opinion that the agency would never succeed, but I say, never allow anyone to determine your destiny and self-worth. I proved them wrong because Dimension Plus Model Agency went on to be an extremely successful venture. Our clients ranged from Saks Fifth Avenue to Glamour magazine, and our gorgeous plus-size models worked for some of the finest fashion houses and magazines in the world. This was about 30 years ago, so I guess you could say that I helped to pioneer the Plus-Size Model fashion world.

To this day, I am still sharing how all of the "not–good-enough moments" in my life have made me the person I am today. In fact, I wanted to contribute to this book for that very same reason. My current career has been fashioned around my desire to help others feel confident in who they are, and I love what I do. I am a speaker, teacher and confidence coach and have helped thousands of people live better lives. Oftentimes, I see people who are very inspired after hearing me speak. It leaves me nearly breathless with gratitude that I am able to positively touch others' lives. I have been called a motivational speaker, but actually, I think motivation comes from within. I am merely a vehicle for the audience to take what I say, feel inspired by it and take action on it, which leads them to a whole new level in their lives.

I've learned that there is a distinct difference between being motivated and being inspired. If I inspire people, it's not from just what I say, but how I say it and the feeling behind it. I truly believe in what I speak about and, as a result, others feel that, too. They say things like, "Wow! That's the same way I feel." "I understand exactly what you're saying." "I can do that, too." On the other hand, in order to motivate someone, you have to offer something that spurs that person to want to achieve a goal. For example, the drive is on for the district manager of the year at a retail store. Within 12 months, eight district managers will focus on their retail stores, provide encouragement to the staff to boost sales and put their best foot forward. The district with the most sales at the end of the 12 months will be recognized with an award.

But as I said, "motivate" and "inspire" are two different things. My goal is to inspire. When I give a presentation and look at the faces of those in the audience, I know I have accomplished what I set out to do. I am thankful for my ability to speak and use "word magic" to captivate people to do things that they may have previously thought were impossible to achieve. When I speak from my heart, I feel gratified when I realize that others are inspired. I view it as a gift and I am happy to be able to share it with others.

Another reason I felt compelled to contribute to this book is because I encounter so many people who say they are not where they want to be in their careers, businesses or lives. I want you to ask yourself this question: "How can I overcome the rejections in my life that hold me back from realizing my goals and dreams?" Does it feel like you should be in another place in your life? Are you someone who possesses the talent, skills and knowledge to achieve success? Perhaps you know that you should have a higher position on your job, or that your sales numbers should be higher. You know that you are in a relationship that is not healthy. You know that your business could be a million-dollar company. There are so many accomplishments that you are capable of achieving, but you haven't gone for it. You want to grow but just cannot seem to start the germination process. The next time that you hesitate with your goals and dreams, think of this quote from Dr. Myles Munroe: "The wealthiest places in the world are not gold mines, oil fields, diamond mines or banks. The wealthiest place is the cemetery. There lies companies that were never started, masterpieces that were never painted. In the cemetery there is buried the greatest treasure of untapped potential. There is a treasure within you that must come out. Don't go to the grave with your treasure still within you." I would add to that "Don't get into a trap of 'I'm not good enough'."

Knowing your purpose can help you realize that you are good enough. Here are five steps to help you determine your purpose and tap into your power.

1. Make a list of your interests. What are your passions? What gifts of talent do you possess? Once your list has been compiled, you will want to determine which of these things you could see as your purpose in life.

2. Ask yourself, "Why do I think this is my future?" Determine the reason you have chosen this for your life's purpose. Decide if you can make a profit. More importantly, discover how this will bring out the best qualities in you.

3. Determine what you need to do to start making your life purpose a reality. Find out what resources are available to help you get started on your journey. Although you have an interest and passion for something, it doesn't necessarily mean that you are

fully knowledgeable in this area. Decide what it is you know and what you need to learn. Does it require going back to school? Or, could you get this information somewhere else?

4. Search for support. Many times, we don't find support in what we assume will be the most likely places. For example, you may believe that your parents or spouse will support you in whatever you want to do. Unfortunately, a lot of times, this is where the negativity in your mind can stem. This is not to say that your family intentionally will try to put your ideas down. Your loved ones may be simply trying to protect you from disappointment; however, their protection is holding you back from trying. You will want to surround yourself with other experts in the area you are pursuing and possibly attend a class the expert is teaching. You can find support in organizations that are within this area, also. I believe everyone should have a mentor, coach and sponsor. Mentors are an excellent support because they realize the difficulties in overcoming your own negative thoughts and will share their experiences with you. Mentors are in a position that you aspire to be. They can share their experiences with you and be a guide to where you want to go in life. A coach supports you, guides you and holds you accountable. A sponsor is similar to a promoter. They "sing your praises" to everyone they meet. In a corporate setting, a sponsor is usually in a position to help you move up the corporate ladder.

5. Determination can be your fuel for motivation. Motivation will be what inspires you to keep going and help you overcome those negative thoughts and the "no's" you receive along the way to an inspired life. Training your mind to keep going, even when you

have been hit hard with rejection, is a powerful tool that will ultimately result in success.

Although these steps may seem simple, it is imperative that you follow them all the way through. Skipping a step could alter how your mind "takes in" the information. You want to first determine what it is you want to do with your life. Decide why this is your purpose and determine a plan to make this happen. Remember, it is important to find a support system that is optimistic and objective. Keep going no matter what obstacles get in your way, including your own mind. Keep telling yourself that you can do this, and you can and will succeed.

DeLores Pressley, *International Speaker and Confidence Coach, is the CEO of DeLores Pressley Worldwide and Founder of the UP (Undeniably Powerful) Woman Network. Her story has been touted in Washington Post, Black Enterprise, Essence, Ebony, and SPEAKER magazines. She is a frequent media guest and has been interviewed on OPRAH and Entertainment Tonight.*

She is the author of five books and has received many awards including Top Ten Business Owners by the National Association of Women Business Owners and an ATHENA Finalist.

DeLores serves on many boards including the O'Jays Scholarship Committee and VP of Operations for the National Speakers Association Ohio Chapter. She is the spokesperson for Humanitarian Hands Charities and Co-Host of radio show; "Wriggling in the Middle" heard on WHBC am. Learn more at www.theUPwoman.com.

Cindy Rack

"Life is a sum of all your choices."

- Albert Camus

Chapter Four
ARE YOU A "VICTIM" OR "VICTOR" OF CIRCUMSTANCES?

*A*s I look back on my life, I realize that I could have allowed myself to be a "victim" many times over, to have a pity party and cry, "Oh, poor me!" I'm grateful that I chose to tell that little "poor me" voice in my head, "Thanks for sharing, but I'm not interested!" Doing so has dramatically changed the course of my life.

I would like to share just a few of the times when I made the decision to be the "victor" and not the "victim", and the positive impact that doing so has had on my career, my children's lives, my finances and, ultimately, my marriage. It's an understatement to say that the stories I'm about to impart would have had very different endings - probably with horrible results - if I had chosen "victim" over "victor." My prayer is that one or more of these stories will resonate with you and encourage you to also make a similar choice.

In the early 1980s, I was working in sales and the only PC on the market was the Apple II. My Uncle Frank had encouraged me to sell computers because they were going to be "the next big thing." After talking with many professional recruiters, however, my hopes were squashed. They all laughed at me because I didn't have a computer science degree and I wanted to sell computers. In fact, I was 21 years old and didn't have any degree, despite that I graduated in the top 40 of my high school class of 642. Back then, I didn't think about attending college, as my parents were blue-collar workers and pursuing higher education wasn't valued as much as finding a good, steady job and working hard.

After facing rejection from recruiters, I could have whimpered away and pursued another career path, but I'm stubborn and I don't like people telling me I can't do something. So I sidestepped the recruiters and started directly cold-calling every calculator and word processor dealer in the Yellow Pages to inquire about a sales position.

"I'll tell you what," one of the owners said. "My sales reps all have computer science degrees because we are going to start selling computers, but they don't know how to sell. If you can teach them how to sell, we'll teach you about computers."

Did he really just say that? I had to pinch myself. That was the start of a successful 25-year IT sales and marketing career that has catapulted me into now owning my own social media marketing business. I shudder to think what would have happened if I chose to be a victim, if I would have thought that I wasn't good enough and settled for a lesser job because I didn't have a college degree.

Years later, I heard a quote by George Bernard Shaw that made me think of that time. "People are always blaming their circumstances for what they are. I don't believe in circumstances. People who get on in this world are the people who get up and look for the circumstances they want and if they can't find them, they make them." That is exactly what I did with my computer sales job.

T. Harv Eker, motivational speaker and author of *Secrets of the Millionaire Mind* said that we are our own sports team. We are the offense, the defense, the owner, the manager, the coach, the fans and the cheerleaders. We should be winning every game! But why aren't we? We are also the competition and we let it win way too often.

During those 25 years in IT sales, life was good. I married and we adopted two beautiful babies. Christina was three days old when we got her; then 21 months later, Anthony was born. (They were from two different families.) My husband, Barry, and I agreed with our daughter's birth family that they could meet when Christina was 18 years old. Then the unthinkable happened: When Christina was seven years old, her birth father called us out of the blue. He had found our names, phone number and where we lived... and he wanted to see Christina. Needless to say, my world was shattered. How could he do that to us? Even though he said that he just wanted to see her, we didn't trust him; after all, he had already broken our agreement by calling in the first place. How could I ever let her out the door again without worrying if he would come and take her?

Barry and I became paralyzed with fear and I was worried that I would instill that fear in Christina. What kind of life would that have been for her? After about a month, I finally said, "Lord, I can't live in fear all the time. I can't be with her every second of every day. You gifted her to us and I'm going to put her at the foot of the cross every day. I trust that you are going to take care of her and protect her when I'm not with her." And so, I have done that every day since. I could have chosen to remain fearful and paranoid. I am so grateful that I didn't. I can't imagine what our lives would be like today if I had given into that fear, especially for Christina. She is now 17 and carefree. By the way, she did meet her birth family recently, including her two half-sisters and three half-bothers. It was a great experience for Christina and it brought everything full circle for her. Barry and I are pleased that it was a happy reunion and we are grateful for her birth parents because if it weren't for them, Christina wouldn't be here!

Something else happened during those 25 years - actually, it's an event that happened to all of us: September 11, 2001. Until that day, Barry and I had considered ourselves to be financially secure and well on our way to a comfortable retirement. Admittedly, we were never very good at understanding the stock market. We just trustingly put in our 15 percent every year and watched our investments steadily grow... until 9/11. WHAM! Four airplanes changed the course of history - for our country, the world and for many of us personally. That day, Barry and I lost a huge chunk of our retirement. We panicked and put it in "safe" stocks and because we didn't understand the stock market, we waited a little too long to reinvest and never really recovered. We were just as emotionally devastated as we were financially. We could have played the victim card, whining and crying about losing our investments and not doing anything about it; however, slowly and steadily for the next three years, we sought a way to recover some of our losses.

It's funny how when you choose to take action, things start to happen. I "stumbled" upon a finance book at the library: *The Prophecy* by Robert Kiyosaki. Hmmm... a book about prophecy... in the finance section? As I turned the pages, it felt like the author was speaking directly to me. He wrote about a potential stock market crash around the year 2015 and cautioned that having one's entire retirement savings in mutual funds could be financially disastrous. (Ouch! That hurt!) He wrote about how real estate is a tangible asset and when people start to lose their houses in an economic downturn, they have to live somewhere, so they rent. Kiyosaki's words got me thinking about rental property as an investment. Two days later, I once again "stumbled" upon a real estate course being offered in my hometown. I knew absolutely nothing about real estate. In fact, I have been known to say, "You will NEVER catch me working in real estate." Ha! In a few short years, Barry and I rehabbed and flipped three houses and we have six rental units. Now when we have to pay college tuition for our children, we say, "We'll just flip another house."

My last story is the hardest to write because in the telling of it, I must expose my heart and be completely vulnerable. About nine years into my marriage, I was disheartened. I had waited a long time to get married and assumed that my reward for choosing my life mate carefully would be deep intimacy - you know, sharing our hopes and dreams together, baring our souls, being close in every way: physically, emotionally, spiritually. That wasn't my reality with my spouse, and I couldn't help but feel like I had been cheated out of a real marital partnership. Those feelings of "poor me" had risen to the surface once more. I felt stuck and I couldn't understand why Barry didn't share my disappointment.

After all, I thought, who wouldn't want to be close to me? I took good care of myself. I was a wonderful Italian cook. I had a decent career. I love watching football and hockey games; for goodness' sake, I even golfed. How many husbands could say all that about their wives? I wondered, *What more does he want? Any guy would give their right arm to be married to me!* (I can laugh about it now, but at the time I was completely serious.) Well, no wonder Barry couldn't get close to me; I was so full of myself, there wasn't any room for him! Once again, I took my concern about my marriage into my daily prayers. And guess what I prayed for? I asked God to change Barry so that we could truly become one. Can you believe that? Not once did I consider that the resolution rested within me and me alone.

Obviously, God had a different plan. One day, He spoke to me in no uncertain terms. The message was something like this: *Cindy, that's enough! You are making an idol out of this!* I laughed and shrugged it off, but every day that week during my quiet time, it kept coming up. I could have chosen to ignore it, but finally I blurted out, "FINE, God! You obviously want me to explore this idol thing. I don't know why. After all, I'm fine. I want to be one with my husband but he doesn't want the same... but FINE, I will explore the idea."

Over the next few months, my conversation with God continued. One day, we had it out in my living room. He exposed my pride and selfishness, as well as the brokenness that both Barry and I had from past hurts and bad decisions. He said to me, *Cindy, I purposely put Barry in your life for a reason. He is a gift and you have not accepted him.* As I finally began to understand this, I yielded to God's guidance. Finally, I was completely willing to sacrifice my pride, resentments and frustrations, to stop being the victim and begin working on becoming victorious in my quest for a fulfilling marriage. "Okay, Lord, you win," I said during a particular instance that brought me to my knees. "If Barry never changes, I will accept him as Your perfect gift. I will put aside my needs and wants for now, and focus on helping Barry be the man You want him to be."

" *Obviously, God had a different plan.* "

What happened next was nothing short of amazing. Barry started to change and, therefore, our relationship began to improve. I know that God wants us to live life abundantly. As it turns out, His idea of "intimacy" in a marital union - the very thing I longed for - is WAY better than anything I could have imagined. Is our marriage perfect? No. As we grew closer in love over the ensuing years, there were times when I would still fight with God and say, "Did you see what he did? Did you hear that?" And God would respond, *Thanks for taking the high road and not thinking of yourself. It will take time. Just be patient.*

If I want Barry to have grace for me when I screw up, then I need to have grace for him. As I look back, God had a much greater plan. He wanted to start a marriage ministry at our church and needed a couple with a testimony. We were that couple. Barry and I had a ministry for five years and counseled more than 25 couples. Many still thank us to this day. If I had insisted on listening to the voice of my "ego" instead of following my heart and surrendering to higher guidance, Barry and I would never have been able to positively influence the lives of other married couples. It was much bigger than us. This experience made me realize that my choices not only affect me, they affect everyone around me. I am aware now that I want to have only a positive impact on others. I want others to be victorious, as well.

So, here are some life lessons that I have learned along the way:

1. I really have to be careful what I think. I've formulated my own quote to remind myself of this: "Feed your thoughts nourishing food because they ultimately become your destiny."

2. When there is a relationship, circumstance or opportunity in front of me, I open my hand and say, "God, You know I really want this. I have (studied, prepared, worked, etc.) to make this happen; however, You know me better than I do. If this is good for me, I know that it will happen because all things are possible with You. If it doesn't happen, then I know it's because something better is planned. I can't wait to see what it is." It helps me to keep things in perspective and look at the future with anticipation instead of worry.

3. I stay away from the naysayers because they only tend to reinforce "victimhood." Surprisingly (or not), some of them can be loved ones who believe they have my best interest in mind, but they are coming from a place of fear. I thank them for their opinions and advice then ignore what doesn't "fit" me and keep moving forward.

4. Circumstances are going to happen in life, good and bad. What makes the difference is how I handle them.

5. Why would I think something positive would happen in a situation or relationship if I respond with a negative attitude? What good comes from blaming and whining? The measure I give out is the measure I get back. It all starts with me.
6. You have to have a vision for your life of the person you want to be and legacy you want to leave.

I would like to close by sharing this powerful thought: The moment you take responsibility for your circumstances is the moment you have the power to change the outcome. Are you going to be the victim or victor? Remember, the choice is always yours.

Cindy Rack, a social media strategist, works with entrepreneurs and businesses to grow their presence on-line using social media. She provides simple yet powerful strategies that can be implemented in just a few minutes a day. Her clients appreciate her relaxed, down-to-earth teaching style and her commitment to excellence.

A life-long learner, Cindy enjoys training with personal and business development leaders. She's an active member of her church and community, serving on the board of directors with Genesis of Pittsburgh, a residential program for pregnant women. Cindy and her husband, Barry, love to golf and invest in real estate. They are lifelong residents of Pittsburgh, Pennsylvania and have been blessed with two children. For more information, visit www.SocialVoiceMarketing.com.

Kari Barnum

"*Go confidently in the direction of your dreams. Live the life you've imagined.*"

- Henry David Thoreau

Chapter Five
A LEAP OF FAITH

*I*magine yourself at the open door of a plane, your parachute ready, and the pilot saying, "It's time." You've made the decision to propel yourself into the great unknown at 13,000 feet. What goes through your mind? On one hand, if you stay in the plane, you will be safe and secure; but if you jump, you might just have the experience of a lifetime. Do you remain safe or do you take the risk of possibly experiencing the ride of your life? I jumped out of a plane at 13,000 feet for my 35th birthday. Apparently, I needed an adrenalin rush to start my next 35 years. Little did I know that less than a year later, jumping into the great unknown would become a metaphor for my life.

Most of us can name a time in our lives when a decision felt that big, a moment in which we knew that the choice we were about to make could transform our lives - for better or worse. What is it that propels us to take that leap of faith and in doing so, change the course of our lives? For some, falling in love, getting married and starting a family takes a leap of faith. For others, changing careers can feel like jumping from a plane. For me, I chose to change just about everything in my life and move to a third world country.

I would love to tell you that in 2005 when I jumped, I knew exactly what I was doing and what the consequences would be. But that would be telling you a story that is not mine. I did take that leap, and it has been both exhilarating and crazy, but it has also brought its share of rough landings. I leapt with the hopes of making a better and more meaningful life for myself and others; yet, like anything in life, there are no guarantees that everything is going to work out fine. That's why it's called a leap of FAITH.

What motivates a person to "jump"? Oftentimes it starts with an inkling that there has to be something more. I had this feeling for years but ignored it. Unfortunately, when we sidestep our gut instincts, it festers into an ache that breeds frustration, longing and discontent. For me, that feeling intensified after I lost my father to leukemia in 2003. I wanted to honor his life by living mine to the fullest but didn't know how. Luckily, I have a God who never gives up and He allowed me to feel that unrelenting internal ache as a wake-up call. Even though at the time I had a great job, owned a house, and looked well put together on the outside, my heart was yearning to do something more meaningful. As most of us know, the heart always wins out!

So in August 2005 when I was 37, I boarded a plane headed for a country that I had never heard of: Burkina Faso, West Africa. I had signed on to be a volunteer with the US Peace Corps, sold my home and everything I owned, said goodbye to everybody I knew. I jumped with only my dream of making a difference. In hindsight, I realize that God had His own plan for me. For four months in Burkina Faso, I lived in a mud hut, peed in a hole in the ground and took bucket baths twice a day to cool my body from the 110-plus degree heat. None of this was a problem; however, I felt useless and due to difficulty with the French language, I struggled to communicate this to my nurse counterpart. So after a visit from a snake one night in my hut, I flipped a coin: "Tails" I go home; "heads" I stay. I flipped it five times and it came up tails four times. So I climbed on my bike and rode until I found a place where my phone got service and I made the call. It was time to go home and although I felt relieved and knew deep down it was the right thing to do, I felt like a failure.

I had jumped and crashed. I asked myself "now what" about 100 times a day and the problem was, I had no idea. I knew that returning to the career I had was something I did not chose to do. My experience in the Peace Corps had definitely shaken me but I still felt called to serve; I was ready to... gulp... jump again. Even with the language barrier in Burkina, if I had medical training, I felt I could have still made a difference. The obvious next step was nursing school. I started an accelerated BSN program and for the next 15 months was consumed with studying and clinical rotations. My dream of returning to Africa sustained me through this rigorous 15 intense months. I graduated the program with honors and passed the nursing boards to become a full-fledged registered nurse. To purse my dream of returning to Africa, I now needed to gain medical experience. I strategically sought out a position as a trauma nurse because I knew it would give me the most amount of experience in the shortest amount of time.

Let me pause to admit that some days I desperately longed for my old life and the stability that it provided.

Change is always difficult. There are rarely major decisions that we make that don't cause us to second guess ourselves. During this time, especially in nursing school, I longed to be more content. Reflecting back, I can say that all the struggles and challenges were worth it. Have you ever felt a calling from God and found yourself resisting? Resisting change is natural but it is necessary for us to become the women who God intended us to be.

After 18 months of gaining experience at a level 1 trauma center, it was finally time for me to jump again. I found myself back on a plane headed for Niger, Africa, another French-speaking country. You might be thinking that I'm a glutton for punishment since I didn't fare well in Burkina with the French language. Well, learning French was definitely an issue but a small one compared to the political problems we encountered there. This chapter is too short to give the details of those nine months but suffice to say that our group was there by invitation of President Mamadou Tandja to replace another American doctor who was retiring. This doctor was working to increase healthcare in the remote village of Maine-Soroa, located a two-day drive away from the capital, Niamey. Maine-Soroa also happened to be the President's home village. The political problems started 10 days after we reached the village and received news that the President had been overthrown and taken out of power by a military force that was now ruling the government. Sadly, all of our "support" was lost and it didn't take long for us to realize that we weren't welcome in this country. So once again, I was back on the plane to the United States long before I was supposed to be, this time even more emotionally battered and bruised than the first experience.

I spent months trying to figure out what had happened

and why. After lots of thought, prayer and introspection, I realized that there was no one to blame. When we are hurt or disappointed, our natural inclination is to strike out and blame others or ourselves. I began to blame myself for making a poor decision, like somehow I should have predicted what would happen. I questioned if I had made another wrong choice in my life. And what was I to do now? Was I even capable of making another important life decision? Finally, I began to understand that there wasn't anyone to blame. Like with anything, time heals and I realized that taking a risk sometimes hurts but the experience is worth it.

So after just seven months back in the United States, I was ready to jump again! Yes, I have been called crazy. My family doesn't even question what I do anymore. Fortunately, three's a charm. I accepted a volunteer position and found myself jumping into the beautiful country of Ethiopia. This time, my goal was to fulfill my agreed-upon contract and stay for the 365 days, no matter what.

Lucky for me, Ethiopia turned out to be a good jump. Kaffinono was the language of the region where I was stationed but fortunately English was the national language. My work was fulfilling and where I lived was one of the most beautiful places I have ever been. Eventually I realized that each time I'd jumped, I was exactly where I was supposed to be. All of these experiences have aided me in understanding who I am and who I am becoming. I am still working on fully accepting this life I have chosen, the good and the bad alike. If I would have known how difficult some parts of it would be, I am not sure I would have taken the same path but I'm sure that is true with everyone. Truthfully, I would not change one second of it. I know that God wants me to walk this path for a reason. I have done things and been places that most people have only dreamt of. I jumped out of my comfort zone and into a totally new world.

Now, ironically, my friends are challenging me to jump out of my comfort zone and stay in States. Funny, my comfort zone has become traveling to Africa. It's not what I would have expected in my life time but it is what has come to pass.

Following one's gut, listening to the heart instead of the head, and deciding to live more on life's edge can be overwhelming, amazing, life changing and fulfilling. It doesn't always feel great. Sometimes you want to quit and live a more "normal" existence. Yet if we are patient, like Sarah in the Book of Genesis, who gave birth in her 90s, the results can be better than we ever expected. Trust me, I am still working on the patience thing! Some days it can still be a challenge to remember all of the blessings in my life and not want to return to my old life. Of course, I know that is not even possible now.

> " *Lucky for me, the third jump was a charm.* "

I pray that I am able to jump many more times before my story ends. What about your story? Have you written it already? Maybe it's time to rewrite what you thought your next chapter would be. Maybe your future includes a jump of your own. Maybe it will be a small one or perhaps it's time to leap big and see the world from a whole new perspective. You might just be surprised at the unexpected path your life takes, and you will probably get more out of life than you ever dreamed. In the end, this is what expanding beyond my comfort zone has meant to me. I encourage you to jump out of your comfort zone. Take a small step or take a big risk and jump! See what God has planned for your life.

Kari Barnum is a registered nurse who has taken her work and passion to provide medical care to remote villages of Africa. She has worked in Niger, Nigeria and most recently, Ethiopia. Kari served as an athletic trainer and college Instructor for 12 years in a university setting prior to becoming a RN. A change in careers has opened up a whole new world and amazing life opportunities. She prays that her life serves as a positive influence on others who are interested in working in third world countries. Currently, Kari resides in California and is working as a pediatric trauma nurse while she plans out life's next great adventure.

Valerie Lipstein

"And the day came when the risk to remain tight in a bud was more painful than the risk it took to blossom."
\- Anais Nin

Chapter Six

DO YOU BELIEVE IN A FRIENDLY UNIVERSE?

*W*e are either pushed by our pain or propelled forward by our vision. In 2004, I was at a crossroad in life and had a choice to make. I no longer loved my chosen career and it was affecting my entire life, including my well-being and my marriage.

We all have choices and can move forward and evolve, or stay in "comfort zone living" and pay the price. It can be painful to stay. I was there eight years ago yet felt too scared and confused to do anything; so I stayed at a job I no longer had passion for. I had been a social worker for about three decades. I dreaded Mondays, lived for Fridays and spent hours numbing out on the couch after work, engrossed in reality TV and wondering how I had gotten this way.

"You can't get out of a prison unless you know you're in one," a mentor once shared. I felt stuck and did not yet understand that my thinking was keeping me a prisoner. If only I could find something I was really passionate about, then my life would be better. My own voice said, "Be grateful for this job. There are many people who are unemployed. Just stick it out until retirement and then you'll have your pension; then things will be fine." Retirement was 12 years away and that thought truly depressed me, yet another year passed before a wake-up call would alter my life forever.

My parents valued safety and security over passion and creativity. Having lived through the Great Depression, they believed in hard work and were not entrepreneurial in spirit. My mother (a teacher) and my father (a company man) both retired with pensions. My father hated his job for 10 years, but stayed. When I was in high school, I dreamed of being a writer or poet and studying at Amherst College where Robert Frost once taught. My parents did not support this dream, as they saw no future in it. I did not argue or attempt to do it on my own; by then I had adopted their values as my own. I choose a state college and a respectable career in social work.

We are always manifesting in our lives. It is our nature. If we look around at the results we have created, then we can begin to see our true beliefs. We manifest consciously or subconsciously by what we put our attention on; eventually, our intentions show up in our lives. Often we manifest unconsciously by focusing on what we do not want.

Back in 2002, I did not yet understand this. That year, I had set a goal to work for the State of Washington. A higher paying job with benefits and a retirement pension sounded perfect. Within a month I heard about a temporary position with the state and applied for it. Two weeks later I was interviewing for the position and got it. I was thrilled. With a $30,000-a-year pay increase and medical/dental for my family, I felt like I had finally arrived. My husband had cautioned me to be careful what I wished for. I liked the challenge and was grateful for the position, but the workload was heavy, fast paced and constantly changing. Services and funds were being cut and the assessments had become longer, adding more to our already intense caseloads. Well, I would make it work. I was 51 years old; retirement was not that far off, I reasoned.

My Wake-Up Call

After two years in this role, I no longer had passion for social work and I began to see the system as flawed. My husband's comment began to haunt me. I felt stuck in a career that I no longer loved, and I would complain to him often. He was getting tired of listening.

Then everything changed the day I received a call that my best friend had died unexpectedly at the age of 52. I was devastated, as I had known Susan since I was 17. We met in the dorm during our freshman year of college and became best friends. We were there for each other through numerous boyfriends, marriages and divorces. We shared laughter, tears, a love of animals and numerous adventures. We could finish each other sentences and people often asked if we were sisters.

In the last four years of her life, Susan was a successful entrepreneur doing work she loved. Prior to that time, she had left a 10-year marriage, finished a graduate program, passed her boards and started her own business. "I am finally loving my life and feel like I'm on the right track," she shared with me. After Susan's memorial service, I reflected on the peace that Susan had found in her life, and it caused me to do some soul searching of my own. I had a choice to make and no matter what the risk, I decided that life was too precious and short to wait any longer.

"Life shrinks or expands in proportion to ones courage," Anais Nin wrote, but I did not feel very courageous. I was scared, with no idea of what to do next. All I knew was that I couldn't numb out anymore. My pain began to push me. Menacing thoughts flooded my mind: *You should just stay at your job, what do you think you're doing? Who do you think you are to leave your job in this lousy economy? You don't have the money to do anything more and your family needs the health insurance.* Then I thought of Susan and another voice firmly whispered, *"You must be courageous."* I listened yet my limited thinking was based on what I had done so far. For months, I went round in circles. I wanted to make a difference in the world helping others, yet that was so general. What could I do?

Shortly afterwards I received an email about life coaching, which I had not heard of before. I felt a resounding "Yes" almost instantly. So within six months of Susan's death, I found my true passion in a new career. It was like walking out of a dark room into the sunlight. I have not looked back since, and I am so grateful and privileged to be able to help women live from their passion.

I often will joke with clients that they don't need to be hit by a two-by-four to get the message that their lives are not on track, yet if they want to learn the lesson that way, they will. We can learn by default or design - meaning, we can get specific about what we want and claim it or just let life happen and go along for the ride. Either way, we will get a result. Each of us has a powerful internal guidance system that sends us signals. When we live by design, we know it. Here's a powerful question that we can ask ourselves, and how we answer will determine how much good we will allow: Is this a friendly universe?

I knew their answer. I was speaking to a group of teenage girls at a dinner event in their honor. Some of them would be leaving the foster care system and going out on their own without families to emotionally or financially support them. Many had spent a good portion of their childhood and teen years in the foster care system, often in multiple homes, some better than others.

"Is this a friendly universe?" I asked. "Albert Einstein said it's one of the most important questions we can ask ourselves." Only one young woman nodded affirmatively, along with the handful of adults who were sponsoring the event.

"Can I share my story with you?" I asked. They nodded and listened attentively. "I felt the way you do when I was younger. I seemed well adjusted yet deep inside I felt disconnected. I thought that if people really knew me, they would not like me and would reject me. I kept others at a distance and felt terribly alone. You see, I too had been raised first in an orphanage then foster care until the age of almost three when I was adopted by an American couple. We lived in England for two years then they brought me to the United States when I was five. I felt that the world was unfriendly and that I could only count on myself.

"That was my core belief, and our core beliefs shape how we do things, what we allow in our lives, who we hang out with and even how successful we become. Yet you and I are born perfect and programmed for mediocrity. We must understand this to have the success we deserve in life. We can change our beliefs once we know what they are; otherwise, they can control us.

"My story is not your story. I realize that many of you have had much more challenging times in a system that is far from perfect. My belief about an unfriendly universe changed in my late twenties when I received a letter that my birthmother had written to the adoption agency explaining the reason why she gave me up for adoption. She was on her own at age 15, when her father kicked her out of their home. Her mother had died when she was born. By the time she gave birth to me, she was barely scraping by in a country that was still recovering from World War II. I began to understand her decision.

"After reading this letter, I cried for days. Then I began the long process of forgiving my birth mother and mending my life. My healing began as I realized that the story I had made up about who I was - unwanted, given up, not worthy - just was not true. Eventually, I stopped holding people at a distance and began to see this world as friendly. Then I finally allowed someone into my life by opening up and sharing my story. He became my life partner. Michael and I have been married for 31 years.

"Our limiting beliefs about ourselves and the world must be uncovered and examined for our true brilliance to shine forth. About 80 percent of our beliefs are formed by the time we are nine years old. We can change our beliefs by telling ourselves another story."

I concluded my talk by saying that the subconscious mind does not know the difference between fact and fiction. Even if we consciously say we want a wonderful partner, for instance, unless we have faith that the universe is conspiring for our good, we may often self-sabotage and feel disappointed in our results.

Three Trances

Do you believe that you have what it takes to live the life you'd love? Do you feel deserving of a great life? Here are three common beliefs that are recurring in my work with hundreds of people that often exist as core beliefs and are disempowering. Perhaps you will see yourself in one of them.

You might think, *I know this, this is nothing new.* I call this the trance of *I've heard this before.* Usually when we are thinking this way, we tune out information. The subconscious mind is so powerful that it can have you believing you know something and therefore do not need to take any action. You will stay in a comfort zone of mediocrity, when all the while magnificence awaits you - but we have to do some deep diving first, not just surface skimming. We need to ask the questions, listen for the answers and look at the underbelly; then we can begin to really live boldly from our inner knowing.

Another common ego defense is the trance of *separation.* You may think, *she does not know what I've gone through. My life has been so difficult and they have it so much easier. She has the money, education or connections that I do not have.* With these beliefs, we are separate from everything and feel that we have to do it all alone. We feel defective, as if something is wrong with us and if people see our flaws, they will dislike us or, even worse, abandon us. This affects us deeper as we become further disconnected from our source, the infinite intelligence in the universe that is omnipresent. When we lose this connection, we truly lose some of our life force.

Lastly, there is the trance of *poverty*. We do not believe that abundance is our birthright, we agree with lack and limitation, and we may even see poverty as somehow more spiritual. We may not be living like paupers by world standards yet we agree with being "good enough" when in fact we are capable of having, being and doing so much more. Instead of living our own amazing life with fine champagne and cake, we settle for a flat cola and crumbs, and live vicariously through others. We tell ourselves that we don't really need that much money to "survive", and we minimize our desires. We use terms like "filthy rich" and "money isn't everything" - all the while missing out on the freedom and gifts that financial abundance can bring us. Worse yet, we stay for years (or even a lifetime) in careers, relationships and situations that invalidate instead of empower us.

The great news is that trances can be broken as we expand in understanding and awareness of who we truly are, and make decisions for what we want. If you are experiencing longings or discontent in your life right now, it is a gift. Those longings and discontent are like beacons illuminating what is possible and informing you that "this is not all there is." If you fail to pay attention, they most likely will not go away. They may come out when you least expect it and may show up in the form of ill health, dire financial issues, broken or strained relationships and problems or dissatisfaction at work. Like a beach ball popping up from the water with great force, you cannot hold them down indefinitely.

First, understand who you really are. You are a precious daughter created from Source itself and therefore a co-creator with infinite intelligence. Spirit makes no mistakes; you are perfect and worthy of great things. Your gift is as unique as your thumbprint; it is yours to discover and no one else could ever express it the way you would.

> " *You are perfect and worthy of great things. Your gift is as unique as your thumbprint.* "

Next, take an honest inventory to see if you are clearly asking for what you really want. Research shows that people who create a life vision for themselves actually live seven to ten years longer and have a better quality of life. Look at these five areas and rate them on a scale of one to five (one being very unsatisfied and five being fully satisfied):

- Career/or creative outlet
- Health and well being
- Financial well being
- Relationships
- Spiritual well being

We all have a choice: We can remain closed and try to drown out the pain with soul-numbing activities and addictions. Or we can decide that it is time to move from fear to faith and live courageously, knowing that we are worthy of every great thing. Yes, there is a risk in living boldly; we will have setbacks and failures. Yet the risk is even greater if we settle for a pygmy life, when we are meant to walk this earth as giants.

In the words of Glade Byron Addams, "Chase down your passion like it's the last bus of the night." Hop on and

take the ride of your life - a life filled with purpose, passion and prosperity - where you believe in the benevolence of the universe and know you are powerful beyond measure.

Valerie Lipstein, *CEO and founder of Inspired Living Now, is a certified coach and life mastery consultant. Her company offers programs for quantum success - assisting small business owners and entrepreneurs ready to up-level their results for greater purpose and prosperity. She is also the founder of Empowering Business Women of Greater Spokane, a unique women's resource and support organization in eastern Washington.*

In addition to her coaching/consulting certifications, Valerie's background includes 30 years of combined experience in social work, law/mediation, and counseling. She holds a juris doctorate and bachelor of arts in social work.

Valerie and her husband Michael are blessed with two amazing adult children. They live in Spokane, Washington with their dog and two cats. Learn more at <u>*www.InspiredLivingCoachingServices.com*</u>.

Carolyn Nava

"For I know the plans I have for you," says the Lord,
*"plans to prosper you, not to harm you, but to give you a
hope and a future."*

- Jeremiah 29:11

Chapter Seven

STRONGER THAN EVER

*W*e all have days that seem perfect: not a cloud in the sky, light breeze blowing, perfect temperature and, for once, nothing seems wrong with the world. In March of 2008, I was experiencing one of those perfect times. I had recently moved my eight-year-old son, Christopher, and me into a perfectly decorated, brand new lakefront condo in Lexington, South Carolina. Our life was peaceful and happy. Life was good.

But sometimes that can change in the blink of an eye. One quiet afternoon a knock on the door startled me. I opened the door and found a South Carolina Department of Social Services case worker with a stern look on her face.

Christopher was visiting his dad and step-mom at their home in Savannah, Georgia, for spring break. She informed me that my ex-husband had reported me as a negligent mother and she had come to investigate. I stood there in shock.

You see, I had been a single mother since my son was 10 months old. Earning the title of sales director with Mary Kay Cosmetics in January 2004 allowed me to be a work-from-home parent. We were so very close. I was actively involved at his school, waited for him at the bus stop each afternoon, and basically lived to be the best mom I could be.

My ex-husband did not put energy into having a relationship with our son over all of those years, and basically saw him a twice a year. He constantly complained that he didn't want to pay child support, and rarely did. As I came to learn, this was yet another classic ploy to get out of paying his "obligation." In his mind, it was less expensive to have Christopher live in his home than to pay child support, and he told me so frequently.

I told the caseworker about his past schemes and threats, but she didn't seem to hear a word I said. She stated that I would not be getting him back during a 60-day investigation. I was so devastated that I couldn't stop crying for the next few months.

As was later confirmed, she falsified my statement on the safety plan that day, which I refused to sign and went on to falsify many reports over the months to follow. Within a few hours of starting the investigation, she faxed the clerk of courts a notice to stop child support. Then, with the blessing of the DSS, my ex-husband and his wife illegally enrolled my son into school in Georgia. As the full-custody parent, all of my rights were violated.

The months to follow were nothing less than total hell.

It became apparent that I wasn't making any progress with the caseworker or her supervisor. They seemed to be convinced that I was guilty. They accepted my ex-husband's accusations, didn't do a proper investigation, and never acknowledged the 35 notarized affidavits that I'd collected to prove that I was an excellent mother.

During the next three months I saw Christopher only once and was only permitted to speak to him on the phone twice. On one of those calls, he told me that at his dad's house, they didn't have anything in the house to eat for breakfast and no money for lunch. He was hungry at school. He also said that his step-mother wouldn't let him drink water because she was afraid he would wet the bed. It took every ounce of my sanity to keep me from going to Savannah and forcibly removing him. I boiled in my bed every night and prayed fervently for God to work on my behalf because I knew I wouldn't be any good to my son if I were in jail for breaking him out of his undeserving prison. The system had failed and it was hurting my son most of all.

People began to wonder about the allegations against me. If they were false, then why hadn't my son been returned? I was deeply embarrassed. The caseworkers treated me like a criminal. I asked God why I was being targeted. During my lonely and sleepless nights, I had time to reflect. I pondered why my life had been so hard up to that point.

I had endured challenges of every kind since childhood: extreme poverty, years of bed-ridden illnesses, feeling unloved and uncared for, terrible depression, anxiety and suicidal times, and surviving most of those years as a single mother with little to no physical or financial support. Wasn't it supposed to be my turn to get a break and live a life filled with happiness and joy that so many people seemed to have? Why would God allow my sweet, innocent son to be put through this? He didn't deserve it. I could handle whatever was thrown at me and would have rather taken a bullet than let him be in harm's way.

My emotional duress led to a downward spiral in all areas of my life. I focused as much as I could on work but being in despair, grief and feeling utterly alone, I could not smile and sell makeup or train consultants as was my job with Mary Kay.

During those torturous months, my precious son was told by his father that I was a bad mother, whom he wouldn't see again until he was 18 and that I would probably go to jail. This caused utter confusion and heartbreak for him.

Thanks to words from a dear friend, I put Christopher's name in a Bible and asked God for his safe-keeping. The mustard seed-sized hope in my darkest hours was that I truly believed that God is just. I had to believe that He wouldn't allow such injustice to prevail.

As a result of the false investigation, the South Carolina Department of Social Services found me guilty without ever bringing evidence before a judge. The verdict was delivered and I was informed that I wouldn't be getting my son back. Although the system let us down, I was not going to quit. My son is the love of my life. After hiring a few different lawyers to fight this outrage, one went to bat for me and eventually, in June 2008 after three tortuous months, Christopher was able to return home.

I am grateful and forever indebted to my attorney. He wrote to the state DSS supervisor about our case, and

immediately my ex-husband was told to return my son and my name was expunged of all of the false charges. The caseworker and her supervisor were found to be at fault. Later, I sued DSS and won the battle after two years of depositions, raw emotions and painful experiences. The caseworker in charge of our case was terminated.

To celebrate my son's homecoming, I threw a big pool party for all of our friends and family to welcome him back. But the son who came home wasn't the same loving child who left. He seemed utterly confused and distant. My heart was broken. It took several months before the loving boy I knew came back around to being close to me.

" Don't quit right before you reach the peak. "

During the months that Christopher was gone, I put all of my time and money into getting him back. Even though I was so relieved to have him home, in the months that followed I couldn't laugh, smile or feel joy. I was having a difficult time transitioning back to our happy lives. Having experienced years of anxiety and insomnia in my early twenties, I relapsed into two more years of health and emotional problems. I found myself unable to focus on work and my income suffered.

Eventually, I was diagnosed with PTSD (post-traumatic stress disorder) and through counseling realized that while being preoccupied with the needs of others, I placed a low priority on my own needs. It was a break-through that finally allowed me to take back control of my life. I began to rebuild my business, slowly but surely.

I found myself on a path of developing my mind and spirit. I surrounded myself with positive people, read good books and listened to inspirational speakers. During this time, I began to date and soon found myself in a relationship. Life was getting back to normal.

Two years later, my beautiful daughter Jillian was born and was diagnosed with ADOA (autosomal dominant optic atrophy) which among other complications causes the nerves to her eyes and ears to fail. There is no cure and not much research is happening because it is rare. She will eventually lose her eyesight and her hearing. This news was devastating. No one goes through a pregnancy planning on giving birth to a child with a difficult illness. This was not the commitment that her father had in mind and he ended our relationship, leaving me to care for her on my own. Thankfully, I was already emotionally and spiritually strong, and while I do have moments of overwhelm, I've learned to put her in God's capable hands.

I've been grateful to be immersed in the Mary Kay culture for almost 13 years. It is an environment in which self-improvement is encouraged, acceptance from peers is strong and we have amazing leadership from strong women. Meeting inspirational women - both my incredible customers and beauty consultants - gave me hope that my daughter and our family could have a hopeful future.

Jack Canfield teaches that no matter the event in our lives, our reaction is all that counts. Taking responsibility is the only thing that will create our desired outcome. During my journey to recovery, I chose to not be a victim. I made the tough choices of surrounding myself with people whom I wanted to be like; other times I was totally alone.

To be a successful entrepreneur again, I had to love myself and find my spiritual center. I had to remember how to dream again because my children deserve to learn from my example. This includes taking care of my health through exercise, eating habits and taking time to pray.

Today, my son is 13 and we are as close as can be. I've chosen to remain a single mom. We don't know to what degree my daughter's disease will affect her. She is an exuberant and loving child and her future is bright. I work daily to raise awareness and funds to find a cure for ADOA.

Today, my belief systems are stronger than ever and focusing on helping others keeps the emphasis off of my challenges. As I support others on their journey to success, I share with them that the people at the top are usually those who have been through more than anyone will ever know.

I say to you, also, that if you've been through a lot and

are in the middle of a bleak situation, persist. Don't quit in the middle, or worse, right before you reach the peak. Take your challenge as a sign that you're meant to succeed because you're not given more than you can handle. You're growing through your journey so that you can inspire others in theirs.

I believe with all of my being that if God plants a dream in your heart, it's meant to happen. Believe in your dreams ardently and go after them. Become an instrument to change lives, and create an incredible legacy along the way.

The reason why I'm blessed to be in the top two percent of Mary Kay's two-million-plus sales force is because I just refused to give up, no matter what circumstances came my way. I have earned many free cars in my Mary Kay career and each of them simply represent the lives that I have been privileged to touch, and hopefully, improve. After all, as my wonderful life coach taught me, our ability to heal and grow defines us, not our titles, incomes or possessions.

I believe that you have that persistence in you, too. Believe that you deserve to live the best life you can, no matter what happens to you along the way. Just keep putting one foot in front of the other, and know that challenges may arise but you will also have the bliss of experiencing those perfect, cloudless days when life is good and all is right in the world.

Carolyn Nava, has been a business owner and single mother for 13 years. She is strategic in supporting and coaching women to be successful entrepreneurs by sprinkling their career in and around their family and faith. Carolyn has been a Mary Kay sales director for nine years and has earned five free cars. Her passion is encouraging women to step into their wildest dreams. She believes that one woman can create a movement, passing her special spark into the lives of everyone she influences. Carolyn lives in South Carolina with her son and daughter, the blessings of her life. Carolyn is a parent advocate who actively raises money to find a cure for Pediatric ADOA. Learn more about Carolyn and support ADOA by visiting www.CarolynNava.com.

Lisa Pustelak

"*Be thankful for what you have; you'll end up having more. If you concentrate on what you don't have, you will never, ever have enough.*"

- Oprah Winfrey

Chapter Eight

YOU WILL FIND WHAT YOU ARE LOOKING FOR

Sitting in the doctor's office on a warm, sunny spring day, anxiously awaiting the results of blood work and other tests, I found myself trying not to worry that something was seriously wrong with me. At the youthful age of 16, I was always physically exhausted, like I could lie down and take a nap at any time. Even after sleeping, I didn't feel rested. This went on for several months. Granted, I wasn't very focused on getting enough sleep. I had an active schedule: school in the mornings, working at my uncle's radio station in the afternoons, and since I planned to skip my senior year in lieu of early college admission, there were universities to visit and applications to be filled out. Summer was coming soon and there would be parties, vacations, trips to the lake and lots of other fun things to enjoy. I just needed to have my energy back, and was anxious for the doctor to give me the results of the medical tests.

What he told me next changed my life in an instant. "Well, we've figured out why you are so tired all the time," the doctor explained. "You have mono and... you're pregnant."

A million thoughts rushed through my mind. Pregnant?
Mono? This just can't be! My parents will kill me. What
about all of my plans? What am I going to do? With
that bit of news, the doctor wrote me a prescription for
prenatal vitamins. "Take these every day. And don't
worry about the mono. It will run its course. I will need to
tell your parents about the pregnancy since you are a
minor, okay?" I begged him to not say anything, and left
his office in a state of shock.

By the time I got home that day, my mom had already
received a phone call from the doctor's office. What I
remember most about our conversation is lots of tears -
from anger, fear and disappointment. I had been dating
my boyfriend, Tom, for a couple of years and while we
should have all seen this coming, my world was suddenly
shattered nonetheless. I feared that my father would
literally shoot both Tom and me but, as it turns out, his
way of handling it was to not speak to me for a few days.
Then that Saturday morning at breakfast, as I opened
a package of toaster pastries, he said, "Just because
you're pregnant doesn't mean you have to eat
everything in the house." That comment stung but it was
far better than getting shot, and the ice was finally
broken between us.

Tom was going to school in a nearby state and usually
came home on weekends. Although we were in love,
I told him right away that he did not have to marry me.
We later decided to at least wait until I was done with
high school. Eventually, both of our families accepted
that a baby was on the way and preparations began.
Naturally, my college plans changed. I applied to a
business school in a nearby city instead, as I knew how
important it was to get an education so I could help to
provide for our baby. I was growing up and starting a

family earlier than planned, yet I was focused on what I wanted to do and believed that I could do it, regardless of what some of my friends and certain family members said. I could not have done it without tremendous support from my parents and grandparents. I started business school in July 1987, a month after finishing my junior year of high school. I moved in with my Uncle Norm and Aunt Paula, who had a home in the city near the school.

My best friend, Merry, was very excited about the baby coming and couldn't wait to find out if she was going to be an "aunt" or "uncle." She would be the baby's god-mother and my maid of honor at the wedding, which was now being planned for the following year.

That summer was a long one but things went well. I was getting good grades at business school and Tom and I continued to meet back home at my parent's house on weekends. That Thanksgiving weekend, we went out for dinner and a movie with Merry and another friend. Merry had suffered from depression in high school and was home schooled during our junior year, so we didn't spend as much time together; then I graduated and was off to business school while Merry was a senior. But ours was one of those friendships in which it seemed like no time had passed since the last time we saw each other. We had a ball that weekend and it was great to see Merry so happy. I guess being back at my parent's house and seeing my high school friends that weekend made me homesick. Very pregnant and hormonal, I wasn't a happy camper being back in the city but Mom assured me that it would pass, and she was usually right. The next day was my Aunt Paula's birthday. When I came home from school that day, I noticed Mom's car in the driveway. I was excited to see Mom and was sure that her visit would cheer me up; however, I knew the minute I walked in the door that we would not be celebrating. Heaviness hung in the air. Then Mom revealed to me that Merry had taken her own life the night before.

The next few days were a blur, although some moments I remember like they happened just yesterday. I felt heartbroken, angry, sad, frustrated, guilty and more. After the funeral, I had no choice but to return to school. Although the pain in my heart was almost unbearable, I knew I had to stay focused on succeeding in school, so life went on. Part of me was looking forward to the life I promised for our baby but another piece of me was looking for someone to blame for Merry's death, and struggling to understand why she would leave me.

Our daughter, Allison, was born on January 21, 1988. In May, I graduated from business school and a month later, Tom and I got married. Those seven months were crazy, for sure, but they would set the foundation for the rest of my life and lead me to many accomplishments. By age 20, I was married for two years, had two children and a house, and was on my way to providing for my family. I worked full time in the accounting field until my youngest daughter, Kristin, was about six months old. Tom was also working full time at a good job, so we decided that I would be a stay-at-home mom. I started selling Avon to earn a little extra money and be around stimulating adult conversation. This is where I met my manager and mentor, Rosemary. She saw traits in me that I didn't. Rosemary taught me to go after what I want, and to be focused, determined and unstoppable. She also introduced me to personal development activities that improved my self-awareness and helped me to realize that I have a choice in everything I think about, feel and do. By believing in me, supporting me and teaching me the things that she had learned to make her successful, she helped me in a big way to launch my own sales career.

After a few years I moved into the cell phone industry, where I spent the next 14 years in sales, management, training and speaking. Finally, I found my passion! I wouldn't be where I am in my career today, running my own speaking and training business, and doing what I love the most, without Rosemary taking me under her wing and helping me find my self-confidence. She taught me to look for my own definition of success and I found it. For me, it's discovering what I love to do the most, that thing I would do whether I got paid or not. It's also choosing to create the life I really want, not letting anyone or anything stop me, and realizing that I am in control of every thought I think.

There have been many times throughout my life when I strayed and found myself looking for what I didn't want, as well. Guess what? I found that, too. One example was the answers I sought to explain Merry's death. It seemed that I was always looking for the pain. Thinking of Merry and feeling bad didn't seem right but I didn't know how else to be. Through my study of personal development, I gained an understanding that there is truly good and bad in everything, and you will find what you're looking for. I realized that I wasn't looking for anything good as far as Merry's suicide was concerned. What could have possibly been good about it? When I changed my mindset and began to ask that difficult question, slowly but surely the answers came. First of all, Merry taught me about friendship. She taught me that true friends could agree and disagree and still love each other through good times and bad. She taught me how to laugh from the depths of my soul. Her belief that life elsewhere is better taught me how important it is to focus on what's good in our lives here on earth. Merry taught me that there is good and bad in everything before I even realized it. Author Wayne Dyer says, "When you change the way you look at things, the things you look at change." When I changed the way I reflected on this time of my life, I was finally able to look forward with resolution in my heart. Merry helped me get to where I am today because of what she gave me early in my life. She gave me my purpose in life: to seek out and take advantage of every opportunity to help people look for all of the good in their lives, and to believe in themselves.

" Finally, I found my passion. "

Today I am grateful for the challenges I have faced and those yet to come because I understand that overcoming them makes me stronger. With the purpose Merry gave me, the confidence Rosemary helped me find, the support of my family and my desire to constantly learn and improve, I am blessed to be pursuing my purpose with passion. I am building my own business with a mission to study and learn, apply that knowledge to my own life and then share it with others through writing, speaking, training and coaching. I created my business, *Belief Builders,* so that I could help others build their self-confidence. Whether I am writing, coaching individuals, speaking at conferences, facilitating public seminars or working with corporate teams, it gives me great joy to teach others that we truly do become what we think about the most. Other people and life circumstances may take from us just about anything we have in our lives, but no one can touch what we think about. I enjoy helping people see that our thoughts determine the results we get in all areas of our lives.

Had I listened to those in my life many years ago who said I couldn't have a baby as a teenager, have a career, and defeat the odds of the massive divorce rates these days, I wouldn't be able to proudly share my story. My two beautiful, successful daughters are now in their twenties, I have a career that I love and thrive in, and a marriage that has lasted happily for almost 25 years as of the writing of this book. Through it all, I remind myself (and help others to understand) that there is always good and bad in everything and you will find what you're looking for.

Lisa Pustelak is a certified life success consultant, the owner of Belief Builders, a professional speaker, trainer and accountability coach. She helps clients create a life they truly desire. Lisa overcame significant personal challenges as a teenager and has enjoyed a successful 20-plus-year sales career. She knows from personal experience that a life full of happiness, love and gratitude is available to you no matter where you've been or where you are now. With heartfelt compassion and a true interest in the success of others, she teaches people to live life as we were all intended to – energetic, happy and full of passion. If you're ready for your dreams to become reality, visit: www.LisaPustelak.com.

Laurie Itkin

"Financial independence isn't about being able to afford fancy cars and designer clothes. It's about knowing that wherever life takes you, you'll be able to invest in the things that matter."

- Laurie Itkin

Chapter Nine

AN ALLOWANCE TO
LAST A LIFETIME

*L*ike many children, my mother received an allowance from her father. Unlike many children, she continued to receive that allowance for a very long time. How long? Until my grandfather died; he was 94.

Throughout my adolescence and teenage years, I experienced great anxiety about my home life. My mother had been divorced twice, and although it was the early '80s, she was still living in the sexual revolution of the '70s. I remember the first time I saw the movie, "Looking for Mr. Goodbar." I recall thinking that my mother was not unlike Diane Keaton's character: a warm, engaging school teacher with a poor body image and low self-esteem.

For several years, my mother went through a string of boyfriends and went out many nights every week. Her priority was to either spend time with a boyfriend, or spend time finding one. Of all my mother's boyfriends, I remember Rodger the most. She seemed to feel proud and privileged to be his girlfriend. He was a handsome marketing executive with a major Pittsburgh department store who drank dry martinis and drove a Datsun 280zx. He didn't move in with us because he was still legally married to his wife, who lived in Florida. When Rodger was diagnosed with melanoma, he moved back in with his wife and children to die. My mother told me after his death that he had "abandoned" her. I wonder if she felt the same emotion when each of her marriages ended.

I had one goal in my junior and senior years of high school: get the heck out of Pittsburgh. I strived for good grades in the most challenging courses offered and managed to get accepted to the undergraduate business program at the University of Pennsylvania's Wharton School. I pursued a business degree because, in my mind, I equated "business" with "financial independence." I vowed never to be dependent on a man for financial security or for my sense of self-worth.

I graduated in 1990 with a University of Pennsylvania diploma in hand, but no job offer. Eventually, I got a job as a financial analyst with a small consulting firm through the woman who had been my "big sister" in the sorority. It was in Washington, DC, required me to work 50 to 60 hours a week and paid $24,000 a year.

After sharing a house with 10 roommates my senior year of college, I desperately needed a place of my own but couldn't afford it. My mother's father ("PopPop", as I called him) offered to pay me a monthly allowance, just as he was doing for my mother. I accepted his offer but felt ashamed. He had already financed one-third of my college education, the amount that I needed after work-study income, grants and loans. It wouldn't be until I was 31 years old that I would pay the last installment in my student loan booklet.

My rent was $635 a month for a 440-square-foot, roach-infested studio apartment. Twice a week I was awakened not by my alarm clock, but by the loud grind of the trash collection truck emptying the dumpster right below my window. PopPop continued to send me a check for my rent every month. Due to the poor economy in 1990, I was laid off just three months after I moved to Washington. I felt even more ashamed.

I found a new job not long after and received a starting salary $4,500 higher than my previous position. I called PopPop with a big announcement: he no longer had to send me rent checks. I had developed a budget and was confident that I could live within my means without his support. He insisted on still sending me a monthly check. I raised my voice and slowly said, "PopPop, I appreciate your generosity but it is no longer necessary." I could hear the sound of his face beaming. This was (and remains) one of the proudest moments of my life.

Looking back, it wasn't the City of Pittsburgh I was trying to escape; it was the confining environment of co-dependence that my mother had created for herself. I suppose that she simply wanted to be "taken care of." I vowed early on to take care of myself. That vision impacted the kind of men I dated, as well as my choice to not have children . It also impacted how I spent and saved money. My mother always knew that if she really wanted something - such as a down payment on a house, new furniture, new carpeting, new clothes or shoes - PopPop would pay for it, and he never disappointed her. Ironically, my mother never felt close to her father, and I believe that is because he always treated her as a dependent, not as an adult woman.

Unlike my mother's parents, my grandparents on my father's side were poor. When my paternal grandmother died, she left me $1,600. Although I wanted to spend that windfall on things that young women like to spend money on, I needed to begin investing for my future. As a young woman, I already knew the difference between "needs" and "wants." I began a self-imposed life course in which I would save up for what I needed and trained myself to minimize my "wants." On January 23, 1993, when I was 24 years old, I took that $1,600 and bought my first shares of stock. I chose Starbucks as my first investment and bought 40 shares at $39 per share.

I dutifully input my cost basis in a spreadsheet which I still update to this day. The spreadsheet has grown quite large and now includes 350 rows of individual stocks, some of which I still hold and others which I sold long ago. With some care and feeding, that $1,600 initial investment grew into a million-dollar portfolio before I hit the age of 40. Although I had worked in the financial industry for only a couple of years, I maintained my dedication to investing, despite changing fields. As I progressed in a public policy and government relations career and my annual salary surpassed the $100,000 mark, I invested more savings into that stock portfolio instead of spending money. I maxed out on my 401k and IRA and always lived below my means. When my company would give an annual bonus, my female colleagues would go on a shopping spree. I stayed home and bought more stock.

The first time my boyfriend Dan (now my husband) came over to my apartment, he announced that I lived "like a college student." He was shocked that I had spent only $10 on a used table to perch my television. I took his comment as a badge of honor. Nearly every night I would log onto my computer, consider placing a stock trade, and watch my investments grow. At that point in my life, it was more important for me to build my future than to spend for today. I wanted the freedom to treat myself to nice things someday, things like European vacations, regular massages and pedicures, and a fully equipped gym. I knew the time would come when I would be able to do that; what I didn't imagine was that it would happen so quickly.

> " *I chose Starbucks as my first investment and bought 40 shares at $ 39 per share.* "

Unlike my friends with staggering credit card, auto and mortgage debt, I don't blink when I now have to spend money for an unexpected emergency. Whether it is hopping on a plane for a funeral, providing medical care for a sick pet, or paying an insurance deductible for a car accident, I don't have to borrow.

With the ubiquity of the Internet, the resources, tools and education for "do-it-yourself" investing are available to nearly everyone, no matter how much money a person earns or has saved. In previous decades, you would call your stock broker, ask him to buy or sell stock for you, and he would walk away from the transaction with a standard $100 commission. Then discount brokers appeared on the scene, allowing you to phone in your order, "talk" to a computer and get charged only $30. Fast forward to this decade and now you can place trades on your computer at $10 a trade or less. Transaction costs for managing your own money are becoming an irrelevant consideration. I believe in a diversified portfolio - meaning that I employ a combination of trading strategies on a variety of stocks and exchange - traded funds (ETFs). My bread-and-butter strategy is "covered call writing," whereby I purchase 100 shares of stock or ETFs and sell one call option tied to that stock. Instead of putting money in a certificate of deposit (CD), money market account or mutual fund, I buy shares of stock or ETFs and sell call options against those assets to not only generate income, but create some protection if the price of the underlying asset decreases.

Many people do not want to take on the risk of the stock market. Unfortunately (or fortunately, depending on how you look at it), with interest rates at historic lows, putting your savings in a money market fund or CD is practically no better than stuffing money under your mattress.

> " *Unfortunately, with interest rates at historic lows, putting your savings in a money market fund or CD is practically no better than stuffing money under your mattress.* "

Sure, investing in the stock market takes a little bit of work, but I would rather have the potential to grow my money even if it requires taking on risk. "Covered call investing" may sound complicated but all it takes is practice. And with certain brokerage firms offering "paper money" trading accounts, you can practice these strategies without risking real money.

After more than 20 years of never taking more than a few days off between jobs, I was laid off at the age of 43. Yet unlike the fear I felt when I was laid off at age 21, this time I felt courageous. I decided to stop climbing the proverbial corporate ladder and instead build a business based on my passion for investing. I launched The Options Lady to inspire, educate and empower other women to become successful, self-directed investors in the stock and options market.

When my stepdaughter Rachel was young, my husband started giving her an allowance. This normal, loving act a father does for his child made me uncomfortable. I wanted to ensure that she didn't take the money for granted like my mother had, and that she would work to one day generate her own allowance. Like most teenagers, she does some babysitting for the neighbors to earn spending money and learn responsibility, but I wanted something more profound for her. I wanted her to feel that sense of empowerment I felt when I learned that I could make investment decisions on my own.

Her father and I decided to seed a Uniform Gift to Minors Act (UGMA) trading account with $1,000, in which she will be able to make one stock trade a week commission-free. We told her that when she turns 18, she will have complete access to the money she has grown (or lost), which she can then use as spending money while she is in college. With my guidance, she is excited to learn how to analyze and select stocks in which to invest. By trading in her own account, Rachel will also experience the risks inherent in the stock market, which will help make her a responsible investor.

Both my PopPop and mother have long passed away, but I know they would be so proud of me for teaching myself, my step-daughter and other women how to become financially independent. In doing so, we can all generate our own allowance, one that will last a lifetime.

Laurie Itkin empowers and educates women to become successful self-directed investors. She is the founder of The Options Lady (*www.TheOptionsLady.com*) and mentors women on how to use stock and options strategies to augment their income. She is also an investment advisor representative with Coastwise Capital Group, an award-winning investment advisor specializing in customized portfolios that combine dividend-paying stocks, ETFs and options. Laurie holds a bachelor of science degree in economics with a concentration in finance from the Wharton School of the University of Pennsylvania. She is a member of the San Diego Women's Foundation and the Hera Hub community for women entrepreneurs. Laurie competes in squash tournaments throughout the country and also practices yoga. She lives in San Diego, CA.

Beth Caldwell

"Yes you CAN do it all; you just cannot do it all at the same time."

- Beth Caldwell

Chapter Ten

NO ONE WALKS DOWN THE AISLE DREAMING OF DIVORCE

I heard a distantly familiar song from the 1980s yesterday: "That's What Love Is For" by Amy Grant. In a flash, it brought back memories of dancing to that same song with my ex-husband just before we were married.

> Sometimes I see you
> And you don't know I am there
> And I'm washed away by emotions
> I hold deep down inside,
> Getting stronger with time
> It's living through the fire
> And holding on we find
> That's what love is for

I remember thinking to myself at that time, *That kind of love is not real. It's not possible...* and at the same time wondering, *IS that kind of love possible?* I pushed the thought to the back of my mind. After all, I was in the middle of planning a big wedding, and as one of the oldest children in my large family, I felt compelled to follow through with my plans because everyone was looking forward to the festivities.

One of my professional mentors recently shared this with me about her divorce: "I married a nice guy but he was the wrong guy for me. " When people ask me what happened to my marriage, I say, "I walked down the aisle to one person, and came back up the aisle with a completely different person." You see, I was under the impression that the person I married wanted the same things in life that I did. Within a few months after the wedding, I realized that I had made a very big mistake. The first time that I decided to leave him was about five months after the wedding. After a frighteningly violent outburst, I packed my car and left. About an hour into driving to no place in particular, I realized that our wedding photos hadn't even arrived from the photographer yet. *How embarrassing to get divorced before the wedding photos are delivered,* I thought to myself. My family would be really disappointed. So, I turned around and went back.

Over the next three years I spent as much time as I could at work and convinced myself that my husband was going through some tough times and would return to his "normal self" once his career got back on track. I put on a happy face with my family, pretending to be okay. I appeared confident at work as an office manager and regional trainer, and received a number of promotions. To the outside world I was always smiling and seemed to have it all. My spouse and I were an attractive couple with a beautiful home, and our lives seemed to be especially perfect when our first son was born.

With a baby in the house, it became harder to pretend that my marriage was "perfect." Friends and family visited more often and I found myself making excuses for my husband's erratic behavior, such as "He's really tired" or "Work has been very stressful for him lately." My bright smile and cheerful disposition were a good cover, but when our second child arrived 19 months later, it became very clear that I would not be able to take care of two babies, a home and a full-time job while shouldering the burden of the BIG LIE. The stress began to show on me. I looked tired, gained weight and my hair had even begun to fall out.

As often happens in situations like this, when a controlling husband finds himself competing with young children, violence escalates. In September 2003, with a 23-month-old and a nine-week-old baby, I packed whatever possessions could fit into my car and drove 400 miles to move in with my parents. For four years leading up to this moment, I worried that they'd be disappointed about my failed marriage. What I discovered was that for four years, they worried that I may never leave him.

After taking a few months to get back on my feet, I moved us into a second-floor apartment in a working class community. Our new place had no washer and dryer, dishwasher or air conditioning, and was very unlike the suburban home on the cul-de-sac that I had just left behind. At first, this did not matter to me at all. I had my freedom once again, and was able to come and go from my new apartment without fear. I fell asleep contented and peaceful that first night. When I woke up the next morning, it was the first time in three years that I didn't find clumps of hair on my pillow.

Being a divorced woman with two very young children was disappointing. I felt lonely and alone, and different from everyone else. It was certainly not what I had planned for my life. I found myself in awkward social situations all the time. People often assumed that I had never been married and would ask me insensitive questions like, "Who are their fathers?" or "Don't you wish you could have a real family?" Sometimes people would talk about me as if I could not hear them. "What a shame." "How sad for her." "It makes you want to count your blessings, doesn't it?"

I didn't seem to fit in socially with any group. My single friends had no children. Married women were intrigued by me but would never invite me to their social outings. I was outgoing, personable, confident and engaging, and I got the sense that they didn't want me around their husbands. Men often found my strength and confidence threatening, and given the independent way in which I navigated life as a single mom, they didn't care to have me around their wives. I decided to become involved in a local church but when I asked to join, I was told that my children were welcome as members but not me; the church didn't permit divorced women.

Eventually I began dating again. I yearned to fit in with my married friends and I desperately wanted to return to the cul-de-sac and have more children quickly, while my boys were still young. If the timing were right, the siblings could be close enough in age and after a few years, maybe no one would remember my big mistake.

Soon I met a man and fell in love. That wasn't hard to do because everyone was so uncomfortable with my situation that I was frequently getting fixed up on blind dates. This man met all the criteria for a perfect husband: good job, house in the suburbs, owner of a minivan and a dog. He was a nice guy but the wrong guy for me. I began to notice that many of his beliefs contradicted mine. He hid them, as many people do when dating. They were small things that would be easy to ignore when dating, but these same red flags would be a real challenge in a marriage. Even though I had made that mistake once before, I was willing to take the risk in order to fit in. Thank goodness, he was older than me and wiser. When he ended the relationship, I was devastated and heartbroken. It took me a long time to recover from this breakup. Years later it occurred to me that it wasn't the end of the relationship that broke my heart, it was the death of my dream of being a happily married mom; because back then, that was my definition of success.

Over the next several years I continued to immerse myself in my work and being a mom. I had lots more blind dates and almost settled for the wrong man a few times. Despite my success in business and parenthood, I still urgently wanted to fit in and be like everyone else. I did the absolute best that I could do for my boys, but we never made it back to the suburbs. I regretted that deeply but always counted my blessings. *Easier isn't always better,* I told myself a number of times. *We don't have a big home with a large yard in the suburbs, but we do have a happy home.*

Eventually, I decided that I would no longer criticize myself for not having a successful marriage. I made a choice to look for real friends instead of the types of people I thought I should be friends with. My perspective changed so that those who didn't approve of me would no longer determine how I felt about myself. My new friends would be individuals and couples that shared my belief system. I wanted to be around others who valued inner happiness more than the model of car they drove, the job title of their spouse, which private schools their children attended and whether their kid's sports teams made it to the state championships.

> " *I discovered that there were lots of fabulous misfits just like me.* "

In making this decision, I discovered that there were lots of fabulous misfits just like me. In particular, I began to notice that many of the women whom I admired the most were not married. In fact, several of them were happily divorced, others were in successful long-term relationships, and a few had never been married. I considered that my path in life was possibly to be forevermore single. Perhaps my outgoing, optimistic personality was just too big to contain and my independence was too much for any man to ever accept.

I also began to observe a few married couples that I admired. These couples simply enjoyed spending time together and did not engage in manipulative, controlling behaviors to get what they wanted from each other. I admired these relationships of mutual respect, but they were rare. When I looked around, I saw mostly unhappy marriages, men and women who settled for what they had and a few rare but lucky couples who were happy. I couldn't understand why some couples were happy and others weren't, so I concluded that there were just not enough good men to go around. That kind of "soul-mate" type of love probably wasn't in the cards for me. Lucky for me, I was mistaken.

Soon after I made the decision to be forever single, I

received a phone call that changed my life. Two of my misfit single friends had given my phone number to a man named Paul and told him that he must call me. I thanked Paul for calling but abruptly informed him that I was too unruly to be tamed and had given up dating. Paul was unfazed by my directness. "Well, have you given up eating?" he asked. I hesitantly answered that I hadn't and found myself having lunch with him a week later.

Paul didn't want anything from me. He didn't need anything from me. He just liked hanging out with me. He liked my sons, too. He didn't care much for my cats at first, but my cats really liked him and I took that as a positive sign. Paul complimented me, and his compliments felt very sincere. He said I was smart, and that he admired me for the difficult choices that I had made in my life. He told me that, with my enthusiasm and positive attitude, I could do anything I wanted.

With his unconditional love and belief in me, I slowly began to feel more comfortable with who I was. Instead of trying to fit in, I began to appreciate that my unique gifts made me stand out. I slowly realized that my life purpose was not to be a suburban wife and mom. I had wasted years trying to become a version of "success" that wasn't really me, instead of nurturing my true self with all of my attributes and abilities.

Miraculously, I found myself in a relationship based on mutual respect and kindness. Like those few beautiful couples that I admired, I genuinely liked being with Paul and respected him for the difficult choices he had made in his life - and he also liked being with me. I realized that the secret to a happy relationship is to never settle. Like many men and women, I had settled early in my life for the wrong relationship because I was in a hurry to have a certain lifestyle, as opposed to just authentically living my life.

> " *I am not pro-divorce.*
> *I am pro-love.*
> *I am pro-you!* "

I've often been criticized for being pro-divorce. For the record, I am not pro-divorce. Divorce is horrible. No one walks down the aisle dreaming of divorce. Yet committing to a person you don't love (or who doesn't love you) is no picnic, and being married to someone who mistreats you is unacceptable. I am pro-love. I am pro-YOU.

> Melt our defenses
> Bring us back to our senses
> Give us strength to try once more
> Baby, that's what love is for

So yesterday, when I heard that old familiar song, I happened to be organizing my closet. I listened closely to the lyrics, thought of my relationship with Paul and how my life with him is organized completely differently than what I could have imagined all those years ago. I smiled, finally knowing the answer to a very important question: Yes, that kind of love IS real. Wait for it. And do not settle for anything less.

Beth Caldwell is a successful entrepreneur, author, TV host and founder of the Smart Business Success Intensive for Women. She owns a public relations firm in Pittsburgh, PA where she specializes in working with small business owners and entrepreneurs. She is a "40 under 40" winner, having been recognized by Pittsburgh Magazine as one of the city's most influential young leaders. She was recently recognized in Washington DC with the national "Radical Woman of the Year" award. Her other books include I Wish I'd Known THAT!, Inspired Entrepreneurs and Get Paid What You're Worth.

Her passion is to help all women succeed in life and business. Learn more at www.BethCaldwellTV.com.

Meredith C. Nealis

"In life you'll realize that there is a purpose for every person you meet. Some are there to test you, some will use you, some will teach you, and some will bring out the best in you."

- Unknown

Chapter Eleven

BECOMING MY OWN LEADING LADY

Sometimes I look back and wonder how I got to where I am today. There have been times when I wasn't sure I was strong enough to make it through, but it is so amazing how my five-year-old daughter, McKenzie Jean, looks at me with her beautiful blue eyes and says, "Mommy, you saved me!" You see, when we are playing together, she is always the princess and I am the one who rescues her from the tower. Yet little does McKenzie know how she saved me. She helped me find someone I had lost along the way: myself. The person I am today is so much more than I ever thought I could be, and I know that she is the little miracle that made that happen.

To know where you are going, you need to know where you have been. The past five years of my life have been consumed with a divorce, the birth of my daughter, the loss of a dear friend, a change in employment, a relationship with a married man, a broken heart, new friends and the miracle of "empowerment." There are so many definitions of that word but perhaps Mahatma Gandhi said it best: "Our greatness lies not so much in being able to remake the world as in being able to remake ourselves."

I have often heard from family and friends that I don't take "no" for an answer, that I never give up on someone even when they hurt me, and that I am stronger than I give myself credit for. What they may not know is that I did give up, briefly. I gave up on myself.

The hardest part has been closing the door to the past and letting go of past hurts, pain, anger, resentment, letdowns, wrong choices and believing in people who didn't believe in me. Moving on has also meant releasing the need to be validated; I had spent my entire life looking for someone to validate me: my parents, friends, ex-husband, past boyfriends. I wasted so much time trying to prove myself to everyone else. I believed that if I did wonderful things for them, they would love me. If I did things "their way" and allowed them to control me, they would love me. If I never said "no" they would love me. Yet in the end, all I felt was less about myself.

In December 2006, I received wonderful news. I was pregnant - finally. After three failed attempts, God had blessed me with my first child. Receiving this news was the best Christmas gift ever. My husband was not as excited as I had hoped he'd be. Naturally, I loved every minute of being pregnant. Being cautious, I waited patiently until the end of the first trimester to share with everyone that our bundle of joy would arrive sometime in August. I felt amazing and thought that nothing could make my life any more perfect. To have a little life growing inside of me was just so wondrous, and this little life has turned out to be even more incredible than I could have imagined.

About the same time that I received this wonderful news, my best friend was diagnosed with liver cancer. Cheryl was beautiful, a devoted wife and mother, and a wonderful friend. She could light up a room. I can still hear her laughter when I close my eyes and think of her. Cheryl was always by my side, and I would stand by hers through the months ahead. The doctors could not operate on the tumor for fear that it would spread the cancer, so the only option was to attempt to shrink the tumor through chemotherapy and radiation. Since I was pregnant, it was not safe for me to be around Cheryl during her treatments, so most of our time together was lengthy phone talks during which we shared our feelings about what each of us was going through in our lives.

By the end of my second trimester, more turmoil came into my life. On the same day that my husband and I learned that our child was to be a girl, he informed me that he was leaving. He no longer wanted to be married and suggested a permanent separation. I was swimming in a sea of uncertain emotions: devastated that my marriage was ending, overjoyed that my precious little miracle was a girl and confounded by my husband's reaction to the news.

I suggested marriage counseling in the hopes of salvaging our union for the sake of our child, but those short-lived sessions only led to more lies and deceit. During this difficult process, I suspected he was having an affair and my suspicions were confirmed with a phone call from the other woman's husband. I filed for divorce, held my chin up, and put my attention on getting ready for the arrival of my daughter. With the help of family and friends, I got the baby's room ready, planned my baby shower and mentally prepared to raise my daughter on my own. When McKenzie arrived on August 22, she was the most beautiful baby I had ever seen, and I fell in love with her on the spot. Gorgeous eyes, perfect fingers and toes... a true miracle of life and so worth the wait.

In a few months, I would divorce, adjust to life as a single mom, change jobs and say goodbye to my dear Cheryl. Before she died, Cheryl got to meet McKenzie. Even though she was heavily medicated because of the pain, she reached for McKenzie's little hand and McKenzie reciprocated with a finger clasp and sweet smile. I will never forget those precious moments. Not a day goes by when I don't think of Cheryl and admire the woman she was.

With McKenzie in my life I had joy sprinkled with loss, heartache and tears. Shortly after the divorce and still feeling vulnerable, I met a man who ended up taking advantage of my frailties. I longed for someone to soothe my soul, to comfort and love me. When I learned a few months into seeing him that he was married and had two young children, I was mad and felt betrayed. But selfishly, I allowed the affair to last about a year due to the feelings I had for him. All the while, I felt guilty because I didn't want to cause anyone the same pain that I had gone through. So, I ended the relationship, feeling more unloved and alone than ever.

Then along came a new man. This relationship caused me to truly change my thinking. You see, when I met this man, I thought I had found a knight in shining armor who was going to rescue me, much like when McKenzie and I play make believe. With this man, I would ride off into the sunset. Boy was I wrong. Instead, this relationship caused feelings from the past to resurface, feelings that I had buried. He was going through a divorce, and spending time with him forced me to relive my own divorce, along with all of the insecurities I experienced at the time. This relationship brought out the "worst version" of me, and I found myself once again trying to fit a square peg in a round hole. I was so focused on making this man happy, analyzing his words and actions, planning surprise trips for him and buying him gifts, and allowing him to drag my heart around. In the end, nothing that I did for him was ever good enough. I became needy and clingy because I was giving so much and getting next to nothing in return. His only reasoning was to say, "I can't embrace how wonderful you are."

The night before my 36th birthday, he broke up with me and broke my heart. The next day, part of me was still sad but another part of me was relieved. I was emotionally exhausted and yet, I tried to analyze what had happened and I blamed myself. After all, I HAD done something wrong: I had made the same mistake again by trying to force someone to want to love me and want to be with me. This is the very definition of insanity: repeating the same mistake over and over again but expecting a different result. I was finally ready to break that unhealthy pattern.

I believe that people come in and out of our lives for various reasons and that everything happens for a reason. I don't always understand the reasons at that time, but I am learning to trust the Higher Power working in my life. I have many wonderful women in my life. My friends are like sisters, always encouraging me and believing in me, as I have done the same for them. As my friend, Trish, always says, "We are amazing," and she is so right. My mom, who is also one of my best friends, has always given me great advice (which I have not always followed). She always says, "Learning life's lessons early is a precious gift. Never forget where you are and where you are going. Dream big, because even if you don't reach the moon you'll still land among the stars."

" No one can rescue me except me. "

My story is one of rediscovering and trusting my inner voice. Though, at times I may have failed to listen to it, that voice has never been wrong. It has guided me through the toughest times and led me to become a better woman, mother, friend and daughter than I've ever been. These past five years have not been an easy road but I needed to take that road because had I not done so, I would have never changed the direction I was going. When everything started to go sideways, I hid behind my job and made it one of my sole focuses. If I wasn't taking care of my daughter, I was working. I used the long hours and late nights working to escape feeling alone. "Feeling" is the key word, as I stopped feeling my feelings and kept myself constantly busy so that I didn't have to be alone with my thoughts. This journey brought me to a place of finally feeling the emotions from my past, learning that I am strong enough to move past them and learning what direction I want my future to take, and to not be afraid of being happy and wanting more for myself and my daughter. These are all still baby steps, but a dear friend once told me, "Change your thoughts; change your life." So now my thoughts center around being with my daughter, new friends, new adventures, finding love, maybe a new job, but definitely a new me.

I believe that if I want things in my life to change, I have to change my thinking. The first change I made was to allow myself time to emotionally heal from the past by remembering that the events that took place served to strengthen my inner self, not weaken it. The second change I made was to start believing in myself again, to see me for who I truly am and to see what everyone around me sees in me, including my daughter. The birth of my daughter was a new beginning for me. Although I may have wandered off the path a bit, these changes have since allowed me to see that I have the power to be, have or do anything that I want. So why settle for anything less than I deserve? Eventually, time heals all wounds.

Most importantly, I've learned that no one can rescue me, except me. I now take time to focus on myself because the true secret to self-empowerment is self-love. In doing so, I can finally be me: a strong, smart, single mom who embraces life, no matter what happens. I have learned that when one door closes, another one always opens.

As Arthur Abbott scripted it perfectly in *The Holiday:* "In the movies, we have the leading lady and we have the best friend. I can tell you are a leading lady but for some reason you are acting like the best friend." I am finally the leading lady of my life.

Meredith Nealis is an author, speaker, positive thought leader and mentor to single moms. She currently works in the mortgage industry as a Senior Loan Officer and has been recognized as a top performer and member of President's Club. She enjoys helping her clients achieve the dream of homeownership and is fondly known as the mortgage originator who won't back down from any challenge. She is a graduate of the University of Scranton. Her passion is to inspire women to believe in themselves and have greater confidence. Meredith lives with her young daughter in Taylor, Pennsylvania.

Cindy Boily

"Don't go through life, grow through life."

\- Eric Butterworth

Chapter Twelve
CHOOSING TO FLY

" W hen is this pain going to stop? No more drugs! I can't take it anymore!" It was another bad day and I was screaming at myself once again. I had been living with a debilitating headache nonstop for four years at this time. Yes, four years, and I had reached the outer limits of my pain tolerance. The pain in my head alternated between something like a pressure chamber blowing its whistle to an intense "brain freeze" that you get from eating ice cream too quickly. This pain is so well explained by David Biro in his book, *The Language of Pain:* It is "an all-consuming internal experience that threatens to destroy everything except itself - family, friends, language, the world, one's thoughts and ultimately even oneself."

In an act of self-preservation, I created a cocoon around myself during those years, only allowing the most essential things and people into my safeguarded world. I was a career woman with a loving husband, three young children, and great relationships with friends and family. I guess you could say I "had it all." My life was in perfect balance. Then the headaches scattered everything out of whack, like a baseball bat smashing a tower of building blocks. I was lost, depressed, overwhelmed and saw no help on the horizon for close to four years. I had to quit my job and give up my career that I had worked so hard for. The smallest of tasks that I had performed so naturally prior to this onslaught of pain now took every ounce of strength I had.

My little ones were only ages four, seven and nine; they did not understand. How could they when even grown, educated professionals had no clue of my daily challenges? I was on a roller coaster with my neurologist, who would write me a prescription and after three months, I would go back for another that was hopefully more effective. After two years of this I realized that my neurologist's plan of action was limited to this roller coaster. Unfortunately, I felt like a lab animal being tested upon for research and my doctors were not listening to me when I told them that the prescriptions were only increasing my torture by adding numerous side effects in addition to the headache pain. This was confirmed one day when he said something that he thought was good news, but I viewed as a death sentence: "Don't worry, Cynthia, we have hundreds of other drug treatments that we can try."

This is not going to be my life! I thought as I walked out of his office that day, blinded by tears. How can I change this? Every time I tried to explain my condition to someone, I would get a look that basically said, "Really? 24/7 headaches? That's not possible." I had the sinking feeling that everyone was questioning my integrity instead of supporting me. I felt alienated and alone, as if I were in the middle of a desert without water to quench my thirst.

Then one day, while trying some alternative treatments in an attempt to leave no stone unturned, I went to see a chiropractor that was recommended by a friend. I entered his office in a zombie state, just going through the motions - that is, until I met the doctor. He struck me as a man with deep compassion. He acted like he had no other patients waiting to see him and, instead, had all the time in the world to listen to my health concerns. As part of his assessment, he ran a scanner down my back and neck that reflected an image on a screen in bright reds, yellows, greens and blues. I was confused by all of these colors but then he turned around, looked at me straight in the eyes and said, "Wow! How do you live with that pain all the time?" Well, imagine a tornado landing in the middle of the desert. *What? He can see my pain?* My mind raced. *I can't believe it!* I don't remember what else happened at that point, only that my eyes filled with tears. I had my guardian angel to thank for getting me home that day because I was in a trance that lasted for days. I returned for treatments twice a week with hope and a lighter step. I could see glimpses of light trying to crack through my self-imposed cocoon. Each time, I went home with blinding pain that started behind my eyes and eventually consumed my entire head, but I figured that it was worth it if he could cure me.

After three months, it was becoming clear that the treatments were not helping. The chiropractor was so convinced that if I would let him continue for 10 more weeks, free of charge, he could get rid of my incessant headache. In the end, I think he was more disappointed than I was; with tears in his eyes, he informed me that there was nothing else he could do for me. Although I tried, I could not adequately express to him that, in spite of not curing my headache, he did help me immensely.

He changed the internal dialogue that I had been struggling with by believing me. He made the invisible visible. I was no longer crazy, and my pain was not "all in my head" - well, literally this is where my pain resided but I was not imaging it. It was real. This was a turning point for me. I walked out of his office floating on air and with a smile on my face. The pain was still present but I had made a choice to no longer suffer.

With a new light shining from within, I vowed to never talk about my pain. I would no longer explain it to anyone and I would do everything in my power to never show any evidence of its existence. That is not to say that I did not at times go into the bathroom, turn on the water in the bath and cry my heart out but from that day forward it did not consume my life. I later found a great Indian tale that eloquently explains my thought process: An old man says to his grandson, "Boy, I have two tigers caged within me. One is love and compassion. The other is fear and anger." The young boy asks, "Which one will win, grandfather?" The old man replies, "The one I feed."

I also incorporated strict pain management skills into my daily routine to help me cope, such as setting up boundaries and reducing my commitments to a level that I could handle without stress. I began to give myself permission to take breaks during the day, eat every few hours and go to bed early to ensure that I had at least eight hours of sleep. To this day, I still live by these rules so that I have energy left for the important things in my life. I felt at the time like I was limiting myself too much, and was not thriving but surviving. It's true that I wanted more. I had always loved my career and missed the daily interactions with adults. I had all of this passion bubbling out of me and wanted to share it. I had a dream of helping people, and thought about returning to school to become a psychologist; however, the sheer thought of the years I would spend in the classroom overwhelmed me even on my good days, let alone when my headaches made it difficult or impossible to concentrate and retain data. Unsure of how much commitment was too much, I started by volunteering at a homeless shelter that had a career center. I helped clients write up their resumes, searched websites and other sources for potential jobs, and coached them about interview skills. It was a great experience. I could set my own schedule and felt that I was making a contribution. It was so inspiring to see clients' eyes light up and their whole demeanor change at the prospect of things getting better in their lives. By helping others, I was hopeful about my own life, and had a peaceful feeling that I had somehow found myself again, too. My cocoon was slowly being peeled away, bit by bit.

During this time, my husband and I had found a private school that we felt would meet the needs of our gifted son who was not being challenged enough. Sending him there would cost a lot more money. I'd had a wonderfully successful career as a credit manager for years before I abandoned it in desperation when I got sick in 1999. The mere thought of going back to work felt like I had a 200-pound barbell weighing me down, so I fell to my knees and prayed: *Please, God, show me a way. If this is something I should do, show me a company that will be flexible with the hours so that I can get back into it.* I had so many doubts! I had updated my resume but was not quite ready to face the challenge. I decided to look online just to see what opportunities might be out there and to calm the demons that surfaced with very logical reasons why I shouldn't get back into the job market. Then a lightning bolt struck me to make sure I got the message right. What I found was a job description that looked like it could have been copied from my previous employment. *I could do that with my eyes closed,* I thought. *Is this a sign? Well, let's test it.* I sent in my resume and shortly afterwards received a call requesting that I come in for an interview the next day. "Oh my God, what should I do?" I asked aloud as I tried to wrap my brain around everything that I would need to set up before I could say "yes" to this position: child care, carpooling, housework, meals... all of those critical voices came at me all at once, but this time I pushed them away.

> " *This time I pushed the critical voices away.* "

Not only did I get the job but the company agreed to my list of demands: a reduced work week, four weeks of vacation every year, and limits on the travel portion of the job. I cannot express the mixed emotions that I went through during this time but I gave myself a pat on the back for facing those fears. I proved to myself that although I struggled every day with pain that was, by then, not only in my head but had also traveled down into my neck and back, I still had a treasure chest of gifts that I could offer those around me. I stayed with that company for more than seven years in the role of credit manager and had great success. I was appreciated by my superiors and when I started talking about making a career change so that I could focus more on helping people grow (I had the opportunity to experience this in managing my team), they suggested that I take on the responsibilities of human resources - or, as I preferred to be called, a "people and culture manager."

While I was acquiring a certificate in HR management, I took my first professional coaching class. I started using the skills I had learned right away in my new role and loved seeing people becoming enthusiastic about their futures. By far, my favorite was when I saw that light sparkle in their eyes when they just realized something that had never crossed their minds before. Unfortunately, this company was acquired by a large corporation, and my role changed to the point where I was no longer interested in it. I hired a coach to help me sort out my options for what I was going to do with my future. I loved the idea of coaching as a profession but one class was not going to fill my toolbox with the skills I would need. So I went back to school, but not the kind of school that required reading textbooks and memorizing a bunch of formulas or statistics. This was about taking my God-given skills of compassion, emotional intelligence, listening, curiosity about people, and my passion for helping people grow. Add in learning a strong foundation of practical coaching skills from the "Harvard of coaching schools" and lots of practice.

During my courses at The Coaches Training Institute, I discovered that although I had changed my internal dialogue, I still had the perspective that I was a victim. I had one more important layer of that cocoon to shed. With my supportive classmates and the amazing coaches who were training us, I made a conscience choice to change that perspective to "this pain experience has opened up doors that I may never have peeked through had it not happened." The best part is that now I get to support and coach those who are going through challenging experiences - be it with their health, career or other life transitions. I can have empathy for anyone who suffers day-to-day, especially with physical pain.

Although even as I write this I am still in constant pain with a persistent headache, and have been since 1999, my life is not defined by it. I still pray for a cure; however, I know deep in my soul that even if I never find one, I can still feel free to fly as high as I'd like in not only my career, but all aspects of my life. And now when clients invite me into their lives, I have the added pleasure and honor of helping them soar, as well.

Cindy Boily *has enjoyed great success during her 20 years in the corporate world in the roles of credit manager and human resource manager. After being coached herself, she discovered her passion to help others reach their goals and full potential. She had always enjoyed that part of her managerial role; however, wanting to concentrate and develop these skills, she quit the corporate world and started training at the Coaches Training Institute (CTI) as a Co-Active Coach®. Cindy is the founder of Butterfly Affect Coaching; she now lives her passion by coaching women who are transitioning to the next chapter in their lives. Living with chronic pain herself, she has a unique ability to relate and empower women who want to thrive and reach their full potential while dealing with the challenges of life. Born in Montreal, Quebec she moved to Calgary, Alberta in 1996, where she enjoys camping and hiking in the beautiful Canadian Rockies with her husband and three children. To learn more visit* www.ButterflyAffectCoaching.ca

Brenda DeCroo

"*As we are liberated from our own fear, our presence automatically liberates others.*"

\- Marianne Williamson

Chapter Thirteen

AROUND THE WORLD AND STRAIGHT TO MY HEART

*L*ife always seemed to come easy for me. Growing up, I was fortunate to have a good family, a comfortable home and lots of friends. Except for some uncertainty as I started out in my career, I wasn't faced with any big life challenges. In my adult life, things continued to be comfortable, stress-free and, yes, "easy"... at least, that's how it appeared from the outside looking in.

After graduating from college with a degree in accounting, I held a number of different jobs - real estate agent, retail manager, outside sales. I just wasn't sure where I really fit in and somehow having a degree didn't make me feel adequately prepared. At age 30, I finally settled into an accounting position and used my degree. I was happy to be able to learn and grow in a respectable occupation. Over the next two decades, I was blessed in many ways. I held several important positions in the company I worked for. I was paid a nice salary - more money than I ever imagined I would earn. And I got to travel all over the world for business. I visited beautiful places and had many wonderful experiences,

113

including attending a military tattoo (band festival) at a castle in Edinburgh, Scotland, and shopping and dining in Old Town Square in Prague, Czech Republic. Two highlights from a trip to Australia were snorkeling at the Great Barrier Reef and attending two performances at the Sydney Opera House. I suspect that others viewed me as a trend-setting, independent world traveler. No one who knew me would have suspected that this seemingly successful woman who appeared to have everything on the outside was crumbling on the inside.

You see, I have always been pleaser, eager to make others happy and make sure they were well cared for. That characteristic contributed to my success, as I had an unending willingness to do whatever it took to accomplish the task at hand. I would gladly step up and tackle each new challenge, and some of these challenges were very important for the success of the company - like installing a global software system and creating a process of controls to satisfy new federal legislation. I would start with excitement, determined to put my creative touch on each project and confident that I would complete the project with brilliant results. But that excitement didn't last very long. A self-deprecating voice would show up in my head: *You might have been able to fool everyone so far, Brenda, but this time you are going to fall flat on your face.* Before I knew it, fear would take over and this voice would taunt me. *Who do you think you are?*

To make matters worse, the projects I worked on were never fully complete. There was always a need for ongoing improvements, better processes, additional reporting; I rarely had that satisfying feeling of accomplishment. One phase of the project would be over, and it was on to the next. The work truly was never done; the demands were unending. I would fall fast asleep each night, exhausted from long, arduous hours in the office, but by three in the morning I would be wide awake, fretting over all that needed to be done. I was always overwhelmed, in a constant state of anxiety, trying to catch up. Of course, I never caught up. *It's all your fault,* that internal critic would reaffirm. *No matter what or how much you do, it is just not good enough.*

Another ongoing conflict for me was that I stayed in this constricting situation for such a long time, even though I had a strong spiritual belief in an expansive and empowering universe. I had been introduced to a new way of thinking shortly after college, learning new concepts like:

- We are souls with a body, not bodies with souls
- We all have within us the power to create our world according to our heart's desire
- We are one with God, each other, and all of creation
- Our thoughts create our reality

I always knew that there was more to my spiritual nature than I was taught in my Catholic upbringing, and this new learning made me feel like some long-captured part of me had been set free. What a mind-opening and expanded way of looking at life! I went on to study these and other spiritual principles with several groups: *A Course in Miracles* and Dr. Pat Jameson's Women's Empowerment group being two of the most profound. I have spent many hours talking with friends, mentors and teachers, sharing stories and affirming the growth that we were all experiencing.

The transformation from these studies was and continues to be a process. Like a spiral, my awareness seems to swirl ever closer toward my inner being, where I feel that oneness and aliveness. But the awareness sometimes seems to shift into reverse, and I revisit those painful lessons that I thought had been learned long ago. A deeper layer of learning emerges as I face again the core issues that I thought I had worked through - lessons like unconditional acceptance of others, patience that the universe will provide, and taking care of myself first. You see, understanding these concepts does not necessarily translate into experiencing them; yet by hearing, reading about and learning these lessons over and over again, the knowledge eventually sinks in and it makes remembering and applying these concepts easier over time.

How could it be that after all these years of experiencing this new way of thinking and having such strong beliefs about what my life could be like, I was still so stuck in a career that was not providing me the joy and fulfillment that I knew was available to me? What was it that made me stay so long and try to fit in while I was having the life sucked out of me?

One of the reasons that I told myself to stay was that I didn't know what I would love to do. I wanted the kind of work that would allow me to confidently express my true self in an authentic way. I wanted to provide value and serve others. Then I started to hear more and more about a new type of service career called "coaching." I learned that a life coach supports individuals who want to be more fulfilled in their lives and have more success in attaining their goals. I started a training program to be a coach and immediately knew that this was something I would love to do every day. I learned the coaching skills to help others get in touch with their strengths and values, to visualize the reality they want in the future, and to make and follow a plan to accomplish their goals. I also learned that I first had to do all of this for myself. So finally, at age 51, I took the time to listen to my heart, to feel what was right for me. I could no longer deny what was pressing on my heart. It was time for change - time to leave this work situation and move onto something that was more aligned with the life philosophies that I so firmly believed in. I made my plans, gave my notice at work and was off to start my own coaching practice.

> " *What made me stay in a job that sucked the life out of me?* "

Funny thing... when I decided to make this change I was fearful that others would ridicule me or think I was foolish. What a surprise when the overwhelming response from coworkers, bosses, family and friends was support, encouragement and admiration. So many others expressed how they would love to step into a life that is more fulfilling. They recognized my courage for following my heart.

For the first time in my life, I have reengaged with who I really am. I now know that I am a strong, loving woman who has much to share, and the universe pulls me to live a life that honors that. Perhaps most importantly, I have come to realize that the foundation for my life's experience, enjoyment and work is "caring", and that the caring must start with me. I care that others are comfortable and free to express who they are in their highest and fullest expression, and this is the life that I have now designed for myself, as well. I know that I must first nurture myself before I can truly serve others.

Finally, I am living an authentic life of serving others. I love coaching! It is a true expression of care for another. When I am coaching others, I recognize the powerful beings that they are, whether they recognize it or not. I hold them in that powerful position as I walk with them for a while down life's path. They tell me of their visions of the destination at the end of the path. They share the joys and longings deep within their hearts and we talk through the "rocks in the road." We sit together on those rocks and sometimes we roll them around a bit to see what they represent. They tell me their fears as we navigate the dark and unknown side trails along their paths; I gently remind them that the power within them will light the way as they go, step by step, in the direction of their hearts' pull.

I know that the conversations I have with my clients are not for their journey alone, for I sometimes still question my path. Am I taking the right steps? Am I moving at the proper pace? Each time I work with a client, I also remind myself of my strength and how my light will reveal my own rightful steps. I know that my journey will continue to grow and evolve, for that is how life works, and that is part of my dream for the future.

So I continue on with trust and caring, paying close attention to what my heart is telling me. I joyfully create the life of my dreams while helping others to do the same. Now, the outside is a true reflection of the inside. I am in total alignment with myself, and from this place of self-confidence and self-nurturance, I can more effectively than ever do what I've always done best: care for myself and others . . . straight from my heart.

Brenda DeCroo, *a business profit coach, works with small businesses and entrepreneurs to increase profits by helping them boost their sales while shrinking expenses. Brenda's clients utilize a powerful but simple system that helps them improve cash flow, experience peace of mind, and finally have time to live their dreams. With more than 20 years of experience in accounting, business development and coaching, Brenda offers her clients a unique and balanced perspective for smart business growth. Brenda is a certified professional coach and holds an MBA from the University of Pittsburgh Katz School of Business. For a free business training video every week, visit www.TheAbundantBusiness.com.*

Pamela B. Losada, MS

"This life is yours. Take the power to choose what you want to do and do it well. Take the power to love what you want in life and love it honestly. Take the power to walk in the forest and be a part of nature. Take the power to control your own life. No one else can do it for you. Take the power to make your life happy."

- Susan Polis Schutz

Chapter Fourteen

FINDING BALANCE, HEALTH AND HAPPINESS BY TAKING CARE OF YOURSELF FIRST

Some people are born with a natural instinct to help others. I am talking about those who would literally drop everything instantly and assist whoever is struggling. I was one such person. As a young adult, I remember wanting to help everyone who could benefit from some kind of support, even if it was just listening and quietly being with them. I didn't help others with the intention to receive something in return. On the contrary, I typically had a difficult time accepting anything in return.

Over the years, I have met many wives and mothers who are exactly the same. We make sure that everyone else's needs are met first: Getting the children ready for school, preparing meals for the family every day, making sure the laundry is clean, working around the house (and in the backyard), and chauffeuring the kids to their various activities. We perform at our best on the job or while building a business. We support a close friend or family member who is struggling with an illness or a relationship issue. When the children get older, we most likely start taking care of our parents in one way or another. At this point in your life, the focus is almost exclusively on others and managing it all day in and day out. This lifestyle might work pretty well for a while, as most women are great at multi-tasking, but are you genuinely happy and full of energy along the way? Most likely not. I knew my energy levels at the time weren't as they were supposed to be. Waking up every morning and not feeling rested was a daily struggle. Feeling sluggish after lunch had become normal. I thought I was happy, for the most part - at least until I actually got to experience what real happiness looks and feels like. Big difference.

As women, we may think we can do it all forever - and we sure can if we choose, but this way of living has its price. Sooner or later, our bodies and minds will make sure we know that we've gone too far and need a break. In my case, it wasn't until I was constantly tired and had some serious health issues that I was prompted to make some real changes in my life. First, I needed to take care of myself, not only taking the time to actually get the proper care and support but also focusing on what I really needed to make my body work at its best, with loads of energy. As Cheryl Richardson writes in *The Art of Extreme Self-Care*, "When we care for ourselves deeply and deliberately, we naturally begin to care for others our families, our friends, and the world - in a healthier and more effective way." This is so true, despite the fact that I believe we all do our best and are pretty successful in assisting others; however, I now know that we can be even more effective without depleting our energy and depriving ourselves of extremely valuable self-care.

You know, taking care of yourself doesn't mean you don't want to help anyone else or be available to others anymore. It is about allowing yourself to live a fulfilling life (both personally and professionally), while being as happy and healthy as possible. Sometimes it means saying "no" to someone (when you usually would drop everything and say "yes") more often than they wish, but that is okay. It is about you and your life. You might find this difficult at first. It certainly was for me. I was often so close to saying "yes" again and again, that I literally had to take a deep breath and a moment to think. You might feel totally out of your comfort zone doing this. In reality, that is exactly what it is: stepping out of your safe, comfort bubble.

In my opinion, putting self-care in your daily routine is a work in progress. It takes time and doing it one step at a time until it becomes second nature. Believe me, it will eventually. It is not about taking a massage here and there, like I was thinking. Don't get me wrong, massages are great but it is also about balancing and nourishing all areas of our lives every single day: for example, nourishing your body with healthy foods, which not only give you the necessary nutrients your body needs to thrive but also the energy to perform at your best. You probably know that if you don't have adequate energy, everything else becomes a hurdle and even relationships can be deeply affected. Self-nourishment also means surrounding yourself with loving, supportive people who simply inspire you to go for what you want, and being in an environment that is judgment- and critic-free. Additionally, you need to love what you do, move your body, be mindful (and be aware of how you feel), and be grateful for what you have in your life. And finally, acknowledge yourself when you accomplish something, even if it is a small achievement. These are all important steps toward an awesome and fulfilling life.

Looking back on my professional life, being a counselor

in Switzerland has been a great experience, although I always felt something was missing professionally in order to support my clients in the best possible way. Moving to the United States, with a stop in Canada in between, I was presented with a great opportunity to follow my passion and add the missing piece for a fulfilling career. Besides helping people, of course, I always had a vivid interest in healthy eating habits and a passion for preparing quick, delicious meals. After my illness and feeling constantly fatigued, I seriously looked at my eating habits. Overall, my predominantly Mediterranean diet wasn't that bad. I made the necessary changes so that I could feel better overall, have more energy and enjoy life much more. Through this experience, I learned first-hand that what and how we eat and drink has an immense impact on our health and well-being. I also learned that the food we give our bodies can actually accelerate or slow down the aging process.

> " *The key is to develop a system that works for you.* "

Armed with this newfound knowledge, I decided to study with world-renowned nutrition specialists at the Institute for Integrative Nutrition in New York City. That life-changing experience is where my new career path as a certified health coach started. I was not only able to improve my personal life and my family's, but now I am able to share my experience and assist others towards their journey to better health and happiness. I use the word "journey" because changes take time and quick fixes don't work long-term. Since our bodies need time to adjust to new ways, I learned that I needed to be patient. I had to trust the process of building new eating and lifestyle habits that work best for my body. Moreover, it was important to understand that not only what we eat, but also how we eat and why we eat the way we do, has a big influence on how we think and feel, our motivation and focus, basically everything. The key to a vibrant, healthy life is to develop your own nutrition and lifestyle system that works best for you. This is the difference between making your new life skills second nature and available to you for a lifetime, and something that works only for a short period of time. Through my education and experience, I have been given the tools to make this transformation happen.

In 2011, I started my health coaching business *The Confident Boomer* from scratch with zero previous experience as a business owner. I definitely stepped out of my comfort zone to follow my passion - not only allowing myself to take care of myself regularly but also by doing everything necessary to do the work I love, and still be able to support other women on their journey to better health and happiness. I now feel more confident and energetic, and more in charge of my health and future than ever before.

I strongly believe that every person has this right and deserves to feel the same way. I also think that every woman has the power to make the first step to move forward and live life on her own terms and stay healthy. As an important first step, you will greatly benefit from aligning with someone who listens and guides you through your journey, and helps you move forward when you would normally feel stuck and frustrated. The right mentor is also someone who keeps you on track and supports you when you get off track now and again (which is totally normal). In short, a good mentor helps you reach your goals.

Remember that it's not about being perfect all the time. (I am a recovering perfectionist, by the way). The emphasis should be on finding balance in all areas of your life. Has my journey been smooth? Of course not. Do I beat myself up? Sometimes. In the past, I would have answered that same question with "always" (typical for perfectionists). Yet along the way, I have learned to take every mistake as a learning experience, as an opportunity to grow and stretch, perhaps more often than I would wish. It becomes easier with time and is so worth it.

I am sure that you, my dear reader, have the potential to put your life back on track and take charge of your health and future. It only takes three things to begin: The belief that you deserve it, the right support and reaching beyond your comfort zone one step at a time. Take that first step today. You deserve it!

Pamela B. Losada, MS (Psychology), is the owner of The Confident Boomer and a certified health coach accredited by the American Association of Drugless Practitioners. She works with women in their late 40s to early 60s who are facing life transitions to help them improve their health and well-being. In her health coaching practice, she develops individualized, step-by-step nutrition and lifestyle plans to help women to have renewed confidence in themselves, and feel more energized and in charge of their health and future. She offers health coaching in person, over the phone and Skype. Additionally, Pamela holds classes, teleseminars and workshops on healthy nutrition and wellness. Learn more at www.ConfidentBoomer.com.

Jennifer S. Ohrman

"Never doubt that a small group of thoughtful, committed citizens can change the world; indeed, it's the only thing that ever has."

— Margaret Mead

Chapter Fifteen

WORTHY OR NOT: HERE I COME! STEPPING OUT OF DOUBT AND INTO "GOOD ENOUGH"

Some people who know me might be surprised to learn of my lifetime struggle with not being "good enough"... but then again, maybe not. As it turns out, I have found many kindred spirits along the way who have grappled with this same issue. I have spent much of my life playing small or "hiding my light under the bushel." The nearly incessant, conflicting mind chatter that has swirled around my brain since I can remember has been an inner battle that has stopped me in my path more times than I can count. When I look back to high school and college, I see so much evidence of others believing more in me than I did in myself. I often sabotaged opportunities given to me because of this deep fear of not being good enough or disappointing others.

Despite this, I have achieved some things that I am proud of. I have always tried to fight my fears (before I learned to bless and release them) and push forward. My family has been my biggest source of inspiration and support. My deep desire for my three children to show up and play full-out in their lives, living joyfully and on purpose, has given me much strength and inspiration to keep growing, release my doubts and fears, and trust that my journey is exactly perfect, even through the darkest times. It is partly through my personal experiences with feelings of depression, anxiety and, at times, grief that helped set me on my path of creating this joyful life that I now experience.

I don't know the exact reasons for my inner struggles with worthiness and not being good enough, but I'll share some insights about myself that may shed some light. Growing up in Northern Jersey, in an idyllic little town, I enjoyed a good childhood and didn't have a care in the world. I was part of a stable, loving family, and had lots of friends and social activities. School was a fun place that I enjoyed going to and my disappointments were few. My naturally optimistic attitude was something I was proud of and throughout my life, people have commented on my positive attitude. That cheerful, optimistic demeanor seemed to be in stark contrast to internal feelings that were, at one point, taking over my life and holding me back from feeling joy, living fully and shining my true light to the world.

A turning point in my life occurred a few years into my career as a physical therapist. I had proudly graduated with honors from Northeastern University in Boston with a degree in physical therapy - a dream come true for me at that moment. However, after several years, what had once been a career I adored gradually became work that no longer filled my soul and was a great source of frustration. In the midst of this, my first sweet baby boy, Jack, was born and I fell in love with him and with motherhood. Almost at once, my desire to be in charge of owning my time and working for myself became... well, some might say... an obsession. My "inner entrepreneur" side, whom I had never met, showed up in a big way and was a catalyst to delve deeper into my personal, spiritual and entrepreneurial growth. During this 15-plus-year quest into my higher self, I have learned as much about others as I have about myself. The revelations have been astounding. In fact, one priceless gift that I have learned to receive from others is the crystal clear - sometimes painfully so - mirror that others who show up in our lives provide for us. One characteristic that had consistently and almost overwhelmingly appeared in my mirror was that of doubt, fear and lack, along with (yes, you guessed it) those relentless thoughts, feelings and behaviors of not being good enough. As I became more aware of my true self, it was a bit of a shock to me that I was filled with such deep feelings of lack and fear, which catapulted me deeper into what has become my perpetual journey of introspection and growth.

While I am able to look back now and see threads of this "not good enough" pattern laced throughout my life, it firmly manifested after college as I began my first career as a physical therapist. While at university, my most significant life-changing event occurred: My beloved mother became ill and passed away from colon cancer. Her death completely rocked my world and changed it forever. She was a mom who deeply believed in my sister and me, and always told us that we could do and be anything we wanted to be, as long as we believed we could. To this day, a favorite memory that brings me back to those feelings of being deeply loved and inspired is the times my sister, mom and I would traipse around the house singing Helen Reddy's *I Am Woman* full blast. Mom was my champion, the one who encouraged me to "roar", as Helen says in her lyrics; losing Mom was devastating but I kept moving forward and, for the most part, I was doing pretty well, staying strong and hopefully making her proud.

" *Mom encouraged me to roar!* "

After graduating from college, I left Boston and instead of moving back to my home in New Jersey, made a side trip to Pittsburgh for my first job (20 years later, I haven't left). I was excited by all the new possibilities in front of me and I welcomed this opportunity for a fresh start. Yet even as I began this new life, familiar feelings of inner doubt began to reappear in new and challenging ways. Soon after the move, I began to feel stress almost constantly. I hid it well, but privately I was freaking out. Always a believer that knowledge is power, I began reading self-help books and soon discovered that I was a poster child for panic attacks, as my feelings of wanting to run and escape certain situations, feelings of my heart beating excessively and more were clearly described in these books as panic disorder. It was a very scary time for me. For someone who has never experienced a panic disorder, it can be very difficult to fathom and even to empathize with. I felt out of control, confused and conflicted. I remember constantly trying to talk myself down from the ledge. My goodness, the mental chatter that was imploding in my head was, at times, almost unbearable. After a while of dealing with the mental confusion, I had learned to plan out every aspect of my life so that I could avoid any possible situation that would set off a panic attack. Needless to say, this was emotionally and physically exhausting, but one of my best traits is perseverance, and I certainly used it during this time in my life.

As I continued to read and research my condition, the

knowledge I was gaining began to comfort me and give me hope. I must have collected every book ever written on anxiety attacks and panic disorder; if I were in graduate school, I could have easily written a dissertation this topic! Part of what I learned is that panic disorders can be treated with medication but my need for independence (or should I say, control?) and strong desire to reject the idea of taking meds kept me from pursuing this option.

Yet I did take the advice of a very good friend - who is, by the way, now my husband of 20 years. He suggested attending a local support group for panic and anxiety disorders. At first, even the thought of attending a meeting nearly sent me into a full-blown attack but I knew I needed to go. For whatever reason, I envisioned sitting in a room with a small group of people who looked nothing like me. So imagine my surprise when I walked into a hotel ballroom packed with people, many who looked quite like me! My fear turned into relief and the rest of the experience was extremely valuable. With love and support from this group, and a deep determination to regain peace and joy in my life, I continued this personal journey into my own healing. I remained open to new information, resources and teachers as they inevitably showed up along the way (and still do). I began to truly appreciate all of my life experiences, pleasant and unpleasant, and finally began to realize that I was not only "good enough" but am more than good enough. All the work I have done to this point has helped me address the unresolved grief that I held onto from my mom's passing, as well as teaching me to embrace the contrasts that show up to guide us and help us to live more purposefully. I still have my moments of doubt and fear, but I now welcome them with love (mostly!) and simply push them aside to choose thoughts and feelings that I like much better.

Today, I am passionate, confident and on most days, filled with joy. Even on the down days, I am really quite good. I run a successful, heart-centered business in the wellness industry helping others make healthier choices for their homes and bodies. I connect with many like-minded souls who deeply desire independence and are determined to serve and make an impact on this world, while creating extraordinary lives together.

I have come to believe that all of me - the light, the dark, the sadness and joy, the love and the pain - is all good, even when it feels bad. Bit by bit, I've come to realize that it was all okay. I am okay. The light had finally begun to shine again and I learned to trust this light. Throughout my journey, I have learned an important truth: We are all good enough. Once I began to doubt my fears rather than doubting my dreams, and learn how to trust this process of life, my light began to shine more brightly, my fears began to shift into possibilities and my doubts became my dreams.

It has been in great part though my challenges and dark times that I have discovered some of life's greatest secrets, one of them being that we can truly create magical and purpose-filled lives no matter (and often because of) what shows up in our lives. I stand today much stronger than before, in my own power feeling worthy, confident beyond measure and damn good enough! I am grateful for each new day and, at times, downright giddy about what the future holds for each of us.

Jennifer Ohrman is a former healthcare professional turned "mompreneur." As the founder and CEO of InPowerMoms.com, she coaches and mentors others to create successful, heart-centered home-based businesses. Jen is passionate about helping women be their own boss, control their time and determine their own worth. She enjoys a thriving business partnership with an Inc. 500 wellness manufacturer, which teams nicely with her extensive personal growth and training background. Jen has been able to effectively and joyfully help hundreds of people create healthier homes, bodies and bank accounts. Learn more by visiting www.InPowerMoms.com.

Tammi Gaw

"Life isn't about finding yourself. Life is about creating yourself."

- George Bernard Shaw

Chapter Sixteen
FINDING MY TRUE COMPASS

*I*t seems like I have spent my whole life trying to find my true compass. I've always been unique and different, and it's been a challenge to establish myself. We live in a society that rewards conformity. I've never really conformed and that makes others uncomfortable. I often receive advice about my behavior, my appearance, and my beliefs and these unsolicited tips can be hurtful. For years, I listened to these "helpful" advice-givers, and allowed my confidence to waver. I wish I had known that it was my prerogative not to listen, and to understand that those who criticized me were mistaken. I wish I knew earlier that my life's direction was my own, and not theirs.

In 1993, I moved from Colorado to Oklahoma to attend the University of Oklahoma. I knew no one there; I had to create a new life in a strange place with new friends. It was not easy, but I emerged with lifelong friends and a career that I could have never imagined. I worked part time as a gymnastics coach at the university's gym, and one afternoon during a team workout, I struck up a conversation with the athletic trainer for the college team. He told me that I could apply for a sports medicine internship, and then structure my coursework to graduate with the necessary requirements to sit for the board exam.

That moment was my first major compass check. I hated the engineering courses I was taking, but I didn't have another option in mind. I just assumed that college was a checklist of courses and then you went and got a job. I had always loved and followed sports, and it never occurred to me that I could work in sports medicine without having to go through medical school. It was the perfect choice for me! Armed with this new knowledge, I changed course and began to work for the University of Oklahoma Athletic Department while pursuing a degree in health and sports sciences.

College graduation brought my next compass check. This time, the compass pointed me west to California. I loved my time in Oklahoma but I was ready to try something new. During a summer camp, I had worked with an athletic trainer who was traveling with a soccer clinic, and he introduced me to a sports medicine clinic just outside Los Angeles. In 1997, I packed up my belongings and found myself driving towards southern California. Later that year, I passed the board exam and began an exciting career as an athletic trainer.

If I'm being honest, I can see many times where my compass got a little turned around. I don't know anyone who doesn't have decisions they regret, and I am no different. There were times when I honestly did not know what steps to take. I experienced betrayal by friends, less than successful relationships, and two quite horrendous living arrangements. Some close friends encouraged me to come back home, but I honestly didn't know where home was. Colorado will always be my first home but, other than my family, there wasn't anything back there that would have made me feel better about life than I did in California. It is distinctly possible that my fear or denial of failing is the only thing that kept me going, but keep going I did. I worked consistently on my athletic training career, and put my extra energy into acquiring a master's degree.

In retrospect, my next move should have probably made me swap my compass for a new model. I loved working with athletes, and some of the best memories of my life are within my career as an athletic trainer. But I didn't know if this was what I saw myself doing for the next 20 years. I wasn't exactly "burned out" but I felt like I needed a change - something less stressful, with more control over my life, perhaps. Well if that's what I was looking for, it makes perfect sense that I should become an attorney, right? Again, many people had plenty of "helpful" advice about my decision to go back to school, but I ultimately had to shut them out and do what I felt led to do and what would be fulfilling for me. So I quit my job, sold my house and started law school. It was a real challenge to be back in school over the age of 30, but I would not change it, even if it meant sitting in a classroom with students who were younger than my youngest sibling.

I was fortunate enough to get a job with an incredible attorney while in school. Without his advice and mentorship, I do not believe I would be the professional I am today. I considered working with him after graduation but I also knew that my career was not going to be that of the typical attorney. I wanted to do my part to change the way corporations act responsibly around the world, and I also knew that I wasn't going to be able to do that in Los Angeles. After a lot of praying and seeking advice, it became clear that the most sensible place to do this work was going to be in the nation's capital.

My move to Washington, DC was by far the most nerve-wracking of all my moves, and not just because I was moving to my fourth U.S. time zone. As I drove across the country, I wanted to turn back more than once. I had been in Los Angeles for 10 years and had three solid communities of friends. I questioned whether I was running from something instead of driving towards something and, believe me, I had plenty of time to mull this over while driving through the endless freeways of Arizona and Texas.

Complete with internal butterflies and an urge to turn back to California, I arrived in Washington just in time for the recession that decimated entire law firms and left thousands of lawyers out of work. I found myself as one of those unemployed lawyers, new to the city and carrying $200,000 in law school loans in my back pocket. During this time, I had some real heart-to-heart talks with my compass, convinced that I had finally made a very, very wrong turn. But even as I doubted my abilities, skills and decisions, I stumbled into a job at a nonprofit where I could do the exact kind of corporate accountability work that I came to DC to do.

I had not envisioned myself working for a nonprofit and it certainly didn't pay the kind of money that I needed. Thanks to the grace of God, I was able to get lower payments that allowed me to stay current on my student loans, but that still took more than half of my monthly net salary. I still pay more per month than I did on my mortgage in California, and almost every one of us knows what a crushing weight debt can be. Washington

140

might not be as expensive to live in as Los Angeles, but it certainly gives it a run for the money. To cut expenses, I had to house sit, rent rooms and occasionally stay in some very generous friends' spare rooms.

During this extremely humbling time, I learned one very key lesson that somehow had escaped me in my previous moves: I had way too much STUFF. I could only keep the necessities with me now as I moved to different houses. Most of my possessions were kept in a storage unit, and I found that it is amazingly easy to part with clutter after only seeing it a few times a year. It is amazing how material possessions can weigh you down, both physically and emotionally. Over the last few years, I gave a lot of it away and had a few yard sales that yielded some much needed cash, but what I earned most in the end was a sense of freedom. I joke now that if it doesn't fit in the back of my Honda next time I move, it's not going with me, and it's almost not even a joke. (I have a very comfortable bed that will certainly require a truck, but the point remains.)

So there I was, in a city that I fell more in love with every day, and doing what I loved at the nonprofit. Most days, I felt very blessed to be doing what I love. I enjoyed my work and had the opportunity to travel to some amazing places. In 2009, I found myself standing in Westminster addressing members of the UK Parliament in London. I bruised my arm from constantly pinching myself. *Could this really be my life?*

It became clear that the transition from Los Angeles to DC was the right move. My compass was aligned, and I was walking on a path more blessed than I could have ever planned. Even with all the success, I had a thought that nagged at me: In the midst of all my moves and transitions, I had always desired to be my own boss. I was now in the land of entrepreneurs, so why not start here? Even with my switch from medicine to law, I never lost my passion for sports, and I just knew there must be a way to merge my skills with sports, law and international work. I discovered that there are fewer than five board certified athletic trainers who are also practicing attorneys, and I am fortunate to call them colleagues, mentors and friends. I decided to start my own company that puts all my passions in one place, and I left the nonprofit at the end of 2011. In 2012, Advantage Rule, LLC was formed.

" *My compass was aligned and I was walking on a path more blessed than I could have ever planned.* "

The name Advantage Rule is a reference to a rule in soccer. It means that when a player on the team with the ball is fouled, the referee can opt to not call the foul so as to not destroy the momentum of the attacking team. To put it simply, it means "to play on through the foul." To name my company after the idea that no matter how many times you get kicked around, you keep driving towards your goal was simply perfect. I felt like it reflected the hard times I had pushed through, and the invaluable teamwork of those around me to motivate me to keep going.

And so my compass has now led me to the latest and possibly most exciting step of my life. There are so many athletes who want to use their money and influence to change the lives of people around the world, and it is the passion of my heart to help them do that in a

sustainable way that engages those they want to help with dignity and with a true heart for service. Advantage Rule has become that vehicle, and I wake up every morning with zeal to make it happen.

At the end of the day, I was born to be individual. And like me, you are also destined to stand out, even if it's only amongst the circle of people around you. We all make mistakes but we learn from them, and we can't let them define us. Some of my regrets have been keys to keeping my compass pointing me to my true north.

My hope for you is that you find your true compass and use it to stay on course, wherever that course may take you. There is no one else just like you, and your course won't always be one that makes sense to other people. I encourage you to stay true to yourself and your passions, and your compass won't let you down.

Tammi Gaw is the founder and executive director of Advantage Rule, LLC, an organization devoted to helping athletes win in the world of responsible philanthropy through sustainable partnerships and dignified engagement with local communities. She has more than 20 years combined experience as an attorney and certified athletic trainer (ATC) which gives her a unique perspective on policies and procedures pertaining to athletes and philanthropy. Tammi is passionate about experiencing life outside of the box, and relishes mentoring young professionals to avoid the trappings of debt and how early financial decisions can lead to freedom and flexibility. Learn more at www.AdvantageRule.com.

Melody Firmani

"What I do today is important because I am paying a day of my life for it. What I accomplish must be worthwhile because the price is high."

- Unknown

Chapter Seventeen

YOU ARE IMPORTANT

I'm not an athlete. I'm not a philosopher. I'm certainly not a genius. What I am is a woman with a song in my heart, a woman who lives life with passion. I've discovered how amazing life becomes when you embrace your God-given gifts and discover your life purpose. When you become driven to share with the world and serve others, you experience the true meaning of life.

Knowing that energy cannot be created or destroyed, I truly believe that the non-physical part of us is very clear about its purpose upon entering the physical world. This material existence brings with it various limitations; some are all around us, and others originate in our minds. Our limiting beliefs can create protective layers that prevent us from acknowledging our true selves. Until we are able to peel away these layers, we will never fully realize who we are intended to be. Many of us survive our lives without allowing our true selves to emerge. We never learn about our gifts and their purpose. We never learn to share them.

When I was born, I am certain that my parents felt the deep love that vibrates down into the soul. Growing up, I knew they wanted only the best for me. Influenced by societal rules, the economic environment and limited emotional resources, however, their parental skills and techniques started the formation of the protective layers that separated me from my truest essence.

We are most fully in our essence before our mind understands language. We are our truest selves before we attach meaning to our daily events. As a toddler, I was a happy- go-lucky child, always smiling, always happy, and always accepting of everyone and anything. Nothing bothered me. I rarely, if ever, got angry and I would not let anything deflate my mood. Every day was an exciting new day. I couldn't wait to get out of bed and enjoy it! I was a peaceful soul, and loved and trusted everyone.

As I grew up, I assigned meaning to everything around me. There were "reasons why" things happened the way they did. For instance, one lesson I was taught at a very young age was that children should be seen and not heard. I was to be obedient and do as I was told. Never, ever speak back your own thoughts or feelings to your parents. The meaning I assigned to this was, "No matter what it is you have to say, it is unimportant. You are not important." I remember my brother receiving a "beating" (this was allowed in my day) because he received a 97 on a school exam and not 100. The meaning I assigned to that incident was, "No matter how well you do something, it is not good enough." What else could I think?

Knowing that my parents did not want to hear what I had to say or care how I felt, I assumed they did not love me. Along with, "No matter what it is you have to say, it is unimportant," "You are not important," and "No matter how well you do something, it is not good enough", my internal conversation included, "If my parents don't love me, who will?" These are not thoughts that develop confidence in a young girl.

My parents were heavily involved in their own dysfunctional relationship and with caring for my down-syndrome sister, and were unable to provide any type of self-esteem building or nurturing care to me, my brother and other sister. I know now that they did the very best they could, but when I was a small child, my immature reasoning resulted in negative thoughts that stayed with me for a very long time.

My early grammar school years simply reinforced these negative thoughts. I was bullied because I was over-weight. My parents didn't allow me to play with other kids after school; instead, I had to complete my homework and practice my violin every day. The reputation of being bullied followed me all the way to my high school graduation. The layers keep getting thicker and thicker.

During my short-lived college days, I started the process of peeling off those layers because I was surrounded by like-minded people with similar goals. My two years at SUNY New Paltz in upstate New York was back in the days of Woodstock, hippies, peace and love. I began to experience the gifts that had been bestowed upon me at birth: peace, love and acceptance of everyone as they are, without judgment or expectation. Another gift was the ability to see everything in a positive light and to help others to do the same. People were drawn to me and loved to talk with me. I did my best to make them feel good and stay positive. I was energetic and optimistic and learned that what I had to say was important. Could it also be that I was important? Imagine that.

> " *Finally, I was surrounded by like-minded people with similar goals.* "

Those short years of personal growth came to a halt when I met my first husband, Nissim. After a very short courtship, a little voice inside told me not to marry this man. There had been many warning signs yet when he said, "You'd better marry me because if you don't, no one else will ever want you," that old, deep-seated thought came rushing back: If my parents don't love me, who will? Afraid that no one else would ever want me, I said yes.

The marriage was rocky from the start. There were two sets of rules: one for him and one for me. His goal was to keep me dependent so I had no choice but to stay with him. I was not allowed to do anything that involved talking to a member of the opposite sex, as he was extremely jealous. He didn't listen to me and if I expressed my feelings about something, his response would always be, "I don't feel that way so you can't feel that way." Once again, what I had to say was unimportant. I was unimportant.

Through my married years more life lessons were learned and more layers were added to my ever-growing protective shield. I was told by my husband, "Don't trust anyone, they are all out to get you." "Everyone is evil."

"The world is not a safe place." "Keep your doors and windows locked at all times." And, of course: "You are not worthy of my attention or of my money."

Fast forward 11 years to the age of 31. I am going through a divorce with my children Danielle, Ivan and Adam, my sister Nicole, and my dad to support and care for. My mother had passed away nine years earlier, leaving behind a three-year-old daughter and a husband. My dad had been diagnosed with manic-depressive disorder and was unable to care for himself or Nicole, so I invited them into my home. I had become his keeper and Nicole's primary "parent." I had also gone back to college and, at the time of my separation, was completing my last semester at Molly College on Long Island, where I was double majoring in music therapy and social work. I was finally on my own after the divorce but I had never had a full-time job. I was fortunate enough to turn my music therapy and social work internships into a full-time position with United Cerebral Palsy in a special educational school for two wonderful years. I loved working with the children, seeing their eyes light up and smiles spread across their little faces every time I entered the classroom. In order to keep up with my bills, however, I had a second not-so-wonderful night job as a receptionist in a physical therapy office. All of those hours away from my children were not helping them, so I decided to seek work outside the social services arena in order to earn enough money to support my family. Who I was and what I wanted to do was unimportant; providing for my family was very important.

I entered the world of financial planning and insurance and did extremely well. I learned the trade thoroughly, created time- and cost-efficient processes, and increased revenue for every company in which I was employed. I was well respected in my field. I also provided motivation to both the sales and support staff. I saw the silver lining in every cloud. When someone had a rough day, Melody was there to set it right. Along the way I developed a "business confidence." Too bad it didn't carry over into my personal life.

That part of my life was hectic, as I attempted to be supermom. No matter what I did, however, the same negative thoughts plagued me. I was alone with my children and my father. While there was support at work, there was none at home, and no one to refute the conversations going on inside my head: You are unimportant. Nothing you have to say is important. You're only going to get hurt.

Fast forward again to age 60, which marked the beginning of my transformation. I have been with my husband, Rick, for thirteen years. My two sons introduced me to a networking/multi-level marketing company. I loved the products and services that were being provided and embraced the concept that with consistent effort, a person can change their financial situation. Even though I had been successful in the corporate world, I still lived hand-to-mouth and I only earned what someone else was willing to pay me. The thought of having a plan B and owning a business that would help others in the process excited me. I wanted to share this discovery with everyone. I wanted to help everyone! While working with one company, however, I found that I was limited to helping only people who saw value in the products and services provided by that one company. I hated the fact that there were people who needed help, but I couldn't help them.

About a year later, I was introduced to Loral Langemeier

and her Live Out Loud community. Loral is all about building wealth but it was through her community that I was able to expand my thinking and identify my gifts. In the Live Out Loud community, surrounded by wonderfully supportive people, I started to realize that the traits I was told to cover up early on were actually my gifts. Imagine that! I was able to be me: energetic, optimistic, caring, giving and supportive of others.

I joined BNI and discovered that "givers gain"; in other words, you have to give without any expectations in order to receive. An amazing concept - one that came naturally to me yet I was once taught was wrong. So one of the layers I let go of was: "You have to expect something back before you do anything."

I joined other networking and professional groups like Pittsburgh Professional Women. Conversations and ideas flowed, support was given and received, and another layer fell away: "No matter what it is you have to say, it is unimportant. You are not important." I started to flourish and began working with my gifts. I felt like I was flying! I love helping people. It's not work; it's a joy. I love supporting others, pairing them up with referral partners or finding them clients. I love turning frowns into smiles. I love helping people believe in themselves. I love that I can just be myself and call it "work."

I had discovered my gifts. Next came my purpose. I had recently presented an "Energy" workshop to clients of a local nonprofit organization. At the end of the workshop, a staff member came up to me and said, "Melody, we need that. Our energy is drained. We give so much to our clients and we get so emotionally involved in their lives that at the end of the day, we have nothing left." Bells went off in my head, and deep vibrations stirred in my stomach and chest. I knew that I was meant to support the caregiver, the individuals who give so much of themselves that they have nothing left at the end of their day. By helping the caregiver who, in turn would better help the care receiver, I would touch the lives of more people. I felt complete.

We are all born with limitless possibilities. We were all meant to be great and to feel this sense of completeness. It is our birthright to live in abundance. It is our purpose to spread energy, optimism and love into the world. We are all unique. Our individual gifts are essential to the evolution of the physical world.

Now, my mission is clear: Embrace myself as I am and live the life I was meant to live - optimistic, energetic, caring, supporting, loving, helping - and share it with others who need it. My heart is full. I am blessed.

Melody Firmani *is a transformational energy coach, author, speaker and entrepreneur. Her unique mission is to move clients from negativity, despair and hopelessness into extreme optimism and energy through motivation, mentoring and education. She specializes in serving the delicate needs of caretakers at senior living, nursing homes and other caregiving facilities throughout the country. Her coaching programs help her clients to discover their gifts, value their vitality and, above all, protect their energy. Melody has studied with personal development industry leaders such as Joe Vitale, Lisa Nichols and Loral Langemeier. She is certified in the Universal Law of Attraction and as a YES! Energy Coach and Consultant. Connect with her at* <u>www.TransformYourEconomy.com</u>.

Mandy Cunningham

"Between stimulus and response there is a space. In that space is our power to choose our response. In our response lies our growth and our freedom."

- Viktor E. Frankl

Chapter Eighteen

THE POWER OF CHOICE

I have to get away from him. That's all I could manage to think as my father shared the truth with me about the life choices he had recently made. The shock of my father's realness and his admitted lack of perfection hit me like a wave. As we drove back to the college campus in total silence, I could see the pain on his face as clearly as he could see mine. The short drive felt like an eternity. Finally, we arrived at my dorm. Reaching my destination was like oxygen in that moment, as if leaving the space that held the words of his choice to betray my mother would somehow stop the changes that had been set into motion.

As he drove off, I couldn't help but feel that my reality for the past 18 years had been a lie. Before this day my life was dependable. My family was solid and strong. My parents were childhood sweethearts. My dad was an involved father and husband and my mother was happy and full of life. Now everything would be different.

I sat on the sidewalk and observed the bustle of activity around me. The sounds of voices and footfall were muffled and distant. I felt separate from the world in that moment. Life was continuing on, despite my confusion. Suddenly I was jolted back to the present, stirred by the sound of my friend Rachel's voice as she walked up to where I was sitting.

"Hi Mandy!" Still distracted, I couldn't respond. "Mandy? Are you okay? Mandy!"

I wasn't okay. My world had shifted. I looked at Rachel and said, "I'll be fine."

That's how life's ups and downs happen, like powerful jolts pushing us in the direction of our destiny. I am not a believer that the "bad cards" we are dealt are single-handedly responsible for the initiation of our success, but more so a lens through which we can see all the possibilities beyond the life we are presently living. Through my life challenges, including the one I just described, I've been able to develop personal clarity by practicing daily my ability to make conscious choices. I will not allow myself to be an individual who leaves my life to chance and identifies with choices made by others.

In the years that followed, my family was surrounded by judgment, gossip and many turbulent changes. I realized that if I was going to thrive in life, I needed to develop a strong sense of self. I envisioned a life of independence in which I followed my own dreams. The secure and stable home that I grew up in had unraveled and the people I depended upon were no longer emotionally available. I began to ask myself, "Where am I going in my life?" This question created a shift in my soul, echoing out a response of possibility and endless opportunity. During this time I learned that I already had everything I needed to live a life that I love. It was not necessary for me to know the "how", "why" and "when."

I spent the next three years focused on my education. I thrived. I did everything a perfect student should do, including the right internships, good grades and exceptional recommendation letters. I graduated with my undergraduate degree and was in line for my dream job as a community outreach manager for a government agency. After six weeks of interviews I thought I had it nailed, but during my final interview I was very nervous and anxious and I blew it - another huge life disappointment that knocked me off my positive-thinking track.

The job market was really tough at that time because of the recession and I faced a difficult choice. I could relocate to another town and work for a large company or stay in my hometown and work for my father. Our relationship was still very strained and working with him was definitely not my dream-come-true. I really wanted to stay in town because I'd started graduate school and had fallen in love with my future husband. I did not want to be far away from my mom and younger brother. I swallowed my pride and accepted the job.

My father was a focused businessman in the office. I received no special treatment. He challenged my limits daily, both personally and professionally. There were many times that I wanted to walk away but my heart would tell me to stay. Our personal relationship remained challenging for the first year. It was not easy for me to work with someone who'd made choices that hurt my family. I often battled with myself and felt torn but I stuck it out. The team grew the company from four to 100 employees in five years. We were named one of Inc. Magazine's 500 fastest growing businesses three years in a row. It was a very exciting time. I enjoyed the challenges and the rewards that came with it.

During this period it became clear to me that a lot of people do not live a life that they enjoy or desire. They base their life choices on what will satisfy others instead of themselves. The experience of my own disappointment, along with seeing others so far removed from the happy lives they had once hoped for, made me resolve once again to make better choices. I reminded myself how valuable it is to identify what I want my life to look like, and not what my parents, friends or society say it should be. I clung to the belief that all experiences, whether positive or negative, would lead me closer to what I had envisioned as my best life.

Having a clear self-vision is the most important lesson I have learned. This shift was a new beginning for me, a lasting one. From now on my choices would be to fulfill my own needs instead of others. I chose to let go of the disappointment about my parents and their trials. Each day became a new step on this path. When I had to respond to a difficult situation, I no longer based my reaction on what others would think or how they would feel. Instead, my choices were based on what felt right for me. I chose a path that served me best, in order to become the woman that I was meant to be, despite the choices and actions of others, and no matter what circumstances I may encounter.

Eventually my father's company was sold. Coincidentally that dream job that I'd blown years before became available at the same time. This time I nailed it. Today I serve and support communities across my home state and work with local and state government officials to improve business operations.

As women, we often make choices based on the expectations of others and our own unconscious thoughts. I've read that we use a mere three percent of our conscious mind to make choices, leaving a staggering 97 percent to unconscious decision-making which is usually based on previous experiences and internal beliefs.

" This time I nailed it. "

When you are faced with change in your life and you feel stuck, overwhelmed, or even devastated, ask yourself, "What do I want?" Then ask, "How do I want to feel?" Think outside of the box with this; you don't want to just be happy, right? Be more specific and remember that your options are limitless. The world will reflect back to you what you send out. If you are harsh and frustrated with yourself, you will probably experience difficulty and hardship. If you are relaxed, kind, open and loving with yourself, you will be rewarded with positive feelings and new opportunities that may have previously been impossible for you to enjoy.

I used to think that when someone disappointed me or hurt someone I loved that the appropriate reaction was to feel disappointed, bewildered or even angry. I now know that this response just attracts more negative feelings. When I allowed myself to feel hurt and angry, I felt worse than ever. Anger can grow when you feed it and if you do, you'll become more upset, hurt and disappointed than you were to begin with. Once I understood this, I knew that I had to stop focusing on my disappointment. Instead, I turned my thoughts to the life I wanted and things began to fall into place.

Today I am attracted to positive things, people and circumstances. The love, stability and fulfillment in my life are all reflections of the clear vision that I've chosen to develop. To enjoy life, I choose how I perceive my circumstances versus allowing my emotions or others to do it for me. We all have the choice to immerse in negativity or bathe in positivity. The world is full of limitless opportunity if you're willing to believe in the power of your choices.

We are brought up in a world that views transition as difficult and conditions us to have fear and anxiety in times of change. I challenge you to look at these times as opportunities. God, the universe or whatever higher form you believe in is clearing a space for you, preparing your life for something new and wonderful to enter. Making the commitment to positive thoughts in times of transition is the only way to allow the experiences to serve you as they are meant to. All encounters and experiences are shaping and refining you for the next moment, allowing you to step onto the stage and walk into shining moments of divine success. Having a clear sense of self will better prepare you for these moments. So, take time to develop your dreams, nurture your passions and determine what is non-negotiable in your life. Define the life that you want to live and hold tight to the path that will produce that life. Challenges, disappointment and heartbreak will happen. When they do, will you be devastated or empowered? The choice is up to you.

Mandy Cunningham is a marketing and lifestyle expert who strives to be an agent of inspiration and positive motion in the world. She is a founder and president of West Virginia Young Professional Women in Energy (YPWE). She holds a masters degree in integrated marketing communications from West Virginia University and has been recognized by Senator Joe Manchin as an example of a successful young professional working and living in West Virginia. Her passion is to inspire women to succeed in life and business. She and her husband reside in north central West Virginia with their dog Bear. Learn more at MandyCunningham.com.

Renee DeMichiei Farrow

"The greatest pleasure in life is doing the things people say we cannot do."

- Walter Bagehot

Chapter Nineteen

FROM COAL TOWN TO UPTOWN

In the small coal mining town where I grew up in Western Pennsylvania during the 1960s and '70s, women weren't expected to do much more than get married, have babies and stay home with the family. My parents, Ray (Tootie) and Eleanor, were first generation Americans of Italian and Eastern European descent. Like others of their generation, they had strong beliefs and customs of how to raise their children. Being the only daughter among three sons - Ray, Randy and Rob - I was treated differently. My dad didn't want my brothers to work in a mill or a mine as he had. He wanted better for them, so the expectation was that they would go to college to make a good living (which they ultimately did). For me, on the other hand, college was out of the question and having something called a "career" was unheard of. The assumption was that I would get married, bear children, take care of my family and never work outside the home. As I reflect on my upbringing, I realize that "I've come a long way, baby," as the Virginia Slims ad slogan once declared.

My early childhood was a happy one. My earliest

memories are of my parents parading me up and down our neighborhood streets every night to visit my Nonna and Nonno, as well as at least two or three aunts and uncles. Mom would always dress me in a pretty starched cotton dress so the neighbors sitting on their porches could marvel at my cuteness. With my curly locks and hazel eyes, I was a little charmer. We would stop at someone's stoop, and in the tiniest voice, I would say, "Hello."

My mother has been a huge influence in my life and, like most parents, she wanted everything for her children that she did not have. Mom had a charitable heart. She would collect money door to door for various charities like Multiple Sclerosis, the American Heart Association, the Leukemia Society and for disabled children. As I got older, it became my job, too, and she taught me by example how to ask for money without hesitation. I also earned my own cash by hosting puppet shows in my basement and picking plums from my neighbor's tree. With all of this "sales" training, perhaps I was destined to one day do something with this skill, although back then, I could never have imagined my future life as a business owner who employs and mentors others.

We lived close to the elementary school, so I walked every day. The cute girl that my mother paraded up and down those same streets was now growing into an awkward, skinny tomboy. With boney legs and arms, and a boyish haircut, the other girls in my class would taunt me with names like Stick, Ostrich and Alice the Goon from Popeye. I wasn't a smart student to begin with and this deeply seared my confidence. I struggled with math and reading, and subconsciously convinced myself that I wasn't "college material," as my parents would agree.

164

Looking back, I remember hating that I grew up in the coal mining town of Renton, with older homes and stay-at-home mothers, instead of a place across town like Holiday Park, where the cool, two-income families lived in modern houses. Again, somehow, this adversely affected my self-confidence.

By the time I entered junior high school, I was on the verge of starting down a dangerous path. Because I was ashamed of who I was and where I lived, I rebelled and got in with the "wrong" crowd. My "friends" and I were into using foul language, fighting when the situation called for it and even experimenting with recreational drugs. Naturally, my grades reflected my horrible attitude. The tables turned and I was the one doing the bullying, calling others names and acting like a "bad" girl.

Thank God I woke up and began to see the light around the end of ninth grade. I had finally grown into my awkward body and cleaned up my attitude. A few of the girls in town noticed that I wasn't Alice the Goon anymore and apparently became jealous. The bullying returned. I was jumped at every corner in town and feared walking to school. Only now that I had more intestinal fortitude from my "bad girl" days, I fought back hard with punches - no biting or kicking or pulling hair for me; I grew up with three brothers! - but these girls still came back for more. My parents were appalled that their daughter was "fighting," even if only for my own self-protection. On one occasion, my dad's response was to beat me with his belt for an incident that involved a knife, although it wasn't mine. My parents decided that I needed to go away for a month before my 10th grade year, so I spent a few weeks at my cousin's home across town to get my head on straight. I enjoyed using their in-ground swimming pool and a cute boy next door caught my eye. Even though he didn't give me a second look, it was a positive few weeks and I wiped my slate clean for the start of a new school year.

Senior high school proved to be a very positive experience for me. My grades improved to the point where I was on the honor roll, I made the basketball team and was captain of the softball team, and even found time to be part of the color guard. My parents' strict upbringing continued; I was not allowed to date, wear makeup or even shave my legs until my junior year. I met a nice boy and we went steady for several years; he had a hugely positive impact on my life. Like me, he excelled in sports and, unlike me, he had his sights set on college. The words of my father kept repeating in my mind: "No daughter of mine is going to college." Most of my female cousins who had ambition had gone on to business school and got jobs - only to (you guessed it) get married, have children and stay home. Maybe I would be different?

After convincing my parents to say yes, I ended up going to a local business school called FPM School of Data Prep. I graduated at the top of my class and was immediately hired by Levinson Steel in Pittsburgh's South Side. So by the time summer was over and my friends were readying to leave for college, I was already a working girl making what I thought was a great paycheck. I was still living at home, so my parents requested that I clean their home as my rent. This was no easy task, as my mom's Slovak roots meant a sparkling clean house that kept a woman busy all week. I was expected to iron on Tuesday, clean my bedroom every Wednesday and the kitchen and bathroom every Friday. This routine actually started for me in fifth grade and I couldn't help

166

notice that Ray (four years older than me), Randy (four years younger) and Rob (six years younger) had only two chores: emptying the garbage and feeding the dogs. But I sucked it up and did what I was asked to do.

On Memorial Day weekend in 1977, I met my husband, Bob, and by Labor Day weekend, we were engaged. By then, I was working at Rockwell International, and Bob's position as a medic for the City of Pittsburgh required us to live in the city, so we found a home in Stanton Heights. I was 19 years old when we married. We planned on waiting three to five years to have children but 18 months later, our son Robbie was born. So yes, initially, I did what was expected by my upbringing: I quit my job, stayed home, took care of my husband and raised the children. We lived on a tight budget and shared one car. We were doing okay.

Three years later we wanted to add to our family. We were ecstatic to learn that we were expecting but I miscarried a few days after Christmas that year. We were devastated but before long, were pregnant again. Our beautiful daughter Rachel was born in February 1984 and our son Ryan came along two years later in April 1986. Our family was complete but all along, I found time to work part time to help pay for Catholic school tuition and other extras for the children. I worked for a local temporary agency and a local steel mill but it still wasn't enough. Using my selling skills, I took the leap into home party sales with Tupperware, House of Lloyd/ Christmas Around the World and Mary Kay. I also signed on with a wholesale fabric/custom drapery business as a phone order entry clerk. My short-term goal was to land a job as a secretary, and I can still remember my mother saying, "Renee, you can't be a secretary! You're a keypunch operator!" Knowing that she was just trying to protect me from disappointment, I responded, "Mom, I can do anything I want to do in this world and I will succeed." And I did. From 1982 to 1993, I worked my way up to sales, design and then marketing. I learned, listened and challenged myself to embrace the interior design business. Then one day, a designer that I was helping spoke these fateful words: "Renee, you have a great eye for design. You should open your own business."

That comment changed my life. I didn't even think twice about it. I just did it, and even my mom was excited. It was November 1992, and I remember filling out the paperwork to register my business on election night. As I watched Bill Clinton give his acceptance speech to become the 42nd President of the United States, I felt inspired that women in this country can do anything they want to; after all, Clinton was married to a powerhouse First Lady. I felt the rightness of my decision and, looking back, it's the best decision I've ever made besides marrying my husband of now 34 years.

I was officially an entrepreneur, and that's a very big word for a small town steelworker's daughter.

I could have never started Decorating Details, LLC without the emotional and financial support of my husband and three children. The summer after I opened the business, my mother's health began to fail and she died in August 1993. After a lifetime of wanting to protect me from overreaching as a woman and risking disappointment, in the end, I know that Mom understood that I would not fail. After all, she and my father taught me to work hard with integrity and honesty. I exceeded their expectations and my own, eventually working with clients across six states, hiring four employees and winning too many awards to list here.

And I didn't stop there. I ran for public office twice - once for Allegheny County Council and a few years later for Pittsburgh City Council. I was invited several times to deliver speeches on behalf of the late Lt. Governor Catherine Baker Knoll, my mentor and friend. Again, I humbly say that for a small town girl who could have taken the "expected" route in life, this was quite an honor. I had successfully traveled "uptown" from my coal town roots.

> *" Renee, you should open your own business. That comment changed my life. "*

Another mentor who helped me do this is Lucille Treganowan, owner of Transmissions by Lucille, a woman who has paved new ground for women in business. The first time I attended a meeting with the National Association of Women Business Owners (NAWBO) after starting my company, I was overwhelmed by all of the successful businesswomen in the room. There I was with only $500 in my business checking account and no experience with running a business. What was I doing? In a moment of panic, I turned to walk out. Lucille noticed the terror on my face and approached me. She invited me to sit at her table and introduced me to other business owners. By the following month, I was lobbying with her in Harrisburg on small business issues. Lucille helped me to realize that every day when I open my door to do business, someone in government is making decisions that will affect me, my employees and my company. She taught me the importance of being involved, which is why I ran for office. Eventually, I served as president and board member of NAWBO, as well as director of the

Commission for Women.

In 2005, after 13 years, it was time to close Decorating Details, mostly because my knees were too bad to continue. After that, I worked for eight years in the advertising department of the Pittsburgh Business Times, then briefly as director of business development for the graphic design firm Zoltun Design. I am currently working in sales for Pittsburgh Magazine. I continue to serve on several boards and am taking classes in leadership and management at a local university. Just as my mother taught me years ago, I still find time to give back to my community. I proudly started the Pauline Eleanor DeMichiei Memorial Scholarship at my alma mater, Plum High School, and my father and brothers have helped to fund this scholarship. To date, we have given more than $12,000 in scholarships to Plum high school graduates.

My true success is my family, and I am proud of them all. Bob is now deputy chief of the Pittsburgh Emergency Medical Services after 37 years of service. Rob works with the Federal Transportation Security Administration and also runs a part-time business. Rachel is an account executive with American Greetings in Cleveland and recently married Andy Swellie. Ryan lives in Haikou, China and works for Schmidt-Curley Design; he just completed his first design for a golf course in Inner Mongolia. At the ripe young age of 26, he has the job that everyone envies and I joke that he is my retirement plan.

As for Dad, I love him so. He remains true to his beliefs, although now I always have the last word. Deep down, I know he respects me for it and is proud of all that I have accomplished. I know that Mom is smiling down on all of us. All told, she and my dad did a fine job raising their four children in a little coal mining town called Renton, which I am proud to call my hometown.

Like any of us, this amazing journey of life has had many ups and downs, failures and successes, tears of sadness and overwhelming joy. What I've learned through it all is that a true leader - regardless of whether it's a man or a woman - faces many obstacles and challenges on the path to enjoying triumphs.

> " *A true leader - regardless of whether it's a man or a woman - faces many obstacles and challenges on the path to enjoying triumphs.* "

As entrepreneurs and employees, we succeed when we have a clear understanding that helping others not only empowers them, it empowers ourselves, as well. I have been blessed with kind and generous female mentors, and it is my continued wish to help mentor other young women and men. If I can make a difference in someone else's life, if I can help another woman see that going from a small town to uptown is not only a possibility but their obligation as a 21st Century woman, then I am a true success.

You see, it's not about who you are, where you came from or even what is expected of you; it's what you do with your one and only life that matters. Yes, I said to my mom many years ago, "I can do anything I want to do in this world and I will succeed." I say that here again, and

I speak for all women everywhere. If you have a dream, don't think twice. "Just do it."

My husband Bob, me, daughter Rachel,
son in law Andy Swellie, oldest son Rob and son Ryan.

Renee DeMichiei Farrow is a lifelong entrepreneur and small business advocate working with clients to market and brand their businesses across the western Pennsylvania region. Past owner of Decorating Details LLC, she has spoken and lobbied nationally on small business issues. Renee has won numerous awards including Pennsylvania Best 50 Women in Business, SBA Regional Women in Business Advocate, YMCA Tribute to Women and Girl Scout Woman of Distinction in Business. She serves on many boards and continues to mentor and give back to her community. Renee's biggest accomplishment is being a wife and mother of three wonderful, successful children who make her life complete. For more information, visit www.ReneeDeMichieiFarrow.com.

Susan Purifoy

"The only way out is through."

- Unknown

Chapter Twenty
LEARNING TO WALK AGAIN

$\mathcal{I}$ didn't hear what the doctor said to my family and friends: "She'll never walk normally again. Driving is out of the question. She won't be able to live alone." Being out of earshot was probably best. I was 41, and had just returned home from a magnificent solo trip to Italy. It was a celebration of my autonomy: re-singled and with a nothing-can-stop-me attitude. Life was great. Yet I would soon learn that life is also unpredictable, out of my control, and that I was about to depend on God in an entirely new way.

Not much compares to falling in a crumpled heap on the floor, just moments after opening my front door. Although I realized that I was on the floor, nothing else seemed wrong to me. My parents, who were there when I fell, saw the telltale signs before I did: Sagging face, mouth misshapen, mental confusion and my insistence that I was "fine." There was also drool. And then the question: "Susan, if you are fine, stand up. Can you stand up?" Of course I could stand up! I could stand up, jump on airplanes, hail cabs and make presentations. I closed deals, raised my children and ran circles around most people. Of course I could stand up... how ridiculous to think otherwise.

Well, there was to be no standing up. My body simply wouldn't comply. I couldn't get my left hand to move voluntarily, and my left leg felt drugged and heavy. All I could do was lean into my dad, who somehow was down on the floor holding me. So, I leaned on him... and many others in the months to come - a new concept for me.

Officially a stroke "victim" at 41, the result of a clot in my carotid artery, my family struggled to remain hopeful in those first hours in the emergency room while praying that I would survive. No one, including me, was concerned at that time with the physical losses that come with stroke. They just wanted me to live. They wanted the doctors to save my life.

I did survive, and my doctor finally talked with me the next day and told me the "truth." My life was changed forever, and there would certainly be significant limits moving ahead, if I could move ahead at all. News like that creates obvious choices: Do you want to fight? Do you have the will to fight? For some, the answer might be resigned acceptance. For others like me, confronted with loss, it's a gauntlet laid down. I had things to do, a life to reclaim, and children to parent. Not drive a car? Not go back to my home? Not acceptable. I would prove my doctor wrong. Watch me.

In the hospital rehab ward, denial looked something like this: I was determined to wear my lipstick even though my mouth wasn't straight, and I assumed I could get out of my hospital bed to walk the five steps to the bathroom. There I was, lipsticked, defiant, and on the floor again, this time on the bathroom tile. I was still Susan on the inside, but my outside was all wrong. I felt scared, lonely and afraid.

I was definitely wounded, and although the "former me" seemed to be missing in action, I can't remember crying or yelling or being furious. I do remember feelings of frustration and powerlessness, accompanied by torrents of fear. And a new, less familiar emotion: embarrassment.

My introduction to victory and shame started when I learned to walk again at 41. My mind knew how to walk, and I certainly wanted to get out of the wheelchair, but my feet didn't seem to remember what they were made to do. Focusing on walking took every single ounce of my grit and determination. I don't think I ever knew real terror until my therapist let go of my legs and urged me to take steps. Those first steps were so difficult, so sweaty, and so completely new. At the time, I referred to my therapists as physical terrorists, but the truth is that they were hope-givers. Told that I could walk, I walked. It wasn't pretty and it wasn't easy, but I walked... past patients and medical staff, all wearing compassion, hope and understanding on their faces. Inside those protective hospital walls, and walking on that rehab floor, I was making my way back to whole. My therapists didn't see me as broken; they saw me as free.

After a month in the hospital, I was released to recover at home, and the world didn't seem to see me as it had pre-stroke, and my perspective had been altered, as well. From my perspective, I was different, and everyone else was different, too. I struggled with stares from strangers, to the point that I wanted to be anonymous. I had always liked it when someone complimented my shoes, my bag or my jewelry. Pre-stroke, I liked being noticed for my eloquence, my ability to negotiate, and even my relationship-style sales approach. I didn't realize the difference between being noticed versus standing out. Post-stroke, I stood out. I no longer had the blessing of blending in. I was a woman with a cane, and I didn't want to be her. I didn't want to be in her body at all.

For much of my initial recovery, I didn't live honestly. To the outside world, I was triumphant and brave, worthy of admiration. In my heart I was scared, insecure and ashamed - ashamed of my new body, embarrassed at needing a cane, critical of how I smiled, terrified that I would never be the same again. I struggled with wanting to hide, but I couldn't. Always a determined woman and in an effort to fight back against the stroke, I decided it best to confront those fears, to test what I could do.

Away from my job for five months, I finally returned, initially part-time and then back to full-time. Within two months, I stubbornly insisted on going on my first solo sales trip post-stroke. Traveling from Atlanta to Chicago alone, the new me struggled and maneuvered, getting where I needed to be, pretending it wasn't all that difficult. It was difficult. It was so very hard. Everything was different; the way I walked, the shoes I wore, walking over a curb, and getting in a cab. Nothing was the same. In this healing were my questions: Could I live this life? Could I figure this out? Looking back on that time, I was trying to show myself that I could recover, that I would return to a normal life. I adopted an overcoming attitude in Chicago, which I now know was the real reason I went.

As a sales manager, I knew about motivation and effort, and was unfamiliar with failure. Stroke recovery was harder than I had anticipated, and I found myself frustrated with my progress. A wounded self-image is not easily slain but repeated effort, over and over, eventually led me to a more realistic and healthy self-view. Work was pivotal in my recovery. The routine of it, the commitment to it, and my colleagues' commitment to me made an enormous difference in my ability to resolve this experience. Although they might not know, their support and belief in me meant everything. My children were also my biggest motivators. The possibility of not returning to live with them, to care for them, to be their mom, was out of the question. Our lives changed dramatically, and we struggled constantly with new realities, but they hung in there, learning with me that life includes devastating losses, as well as impossible joy. God was still good, no matter how dark the day. There was a purpose to this pain. I was sure of it.

> *"To the outside world I was triumphant and brave, but inside I was scared, insecure and ashamed."*

The biggest foe in my recovery was, and 11 years later still is, my mind. Fear blinds me sometimes, keeping me locked in paralysis. Fear is a giant. It is nearly always irrational, threatening to keep me from confidently descending the stairs, crossing a street or attending an event. Conversely, the greatest tool I have in my healing is also my mind. If my brain can create new pathways to direct my feet to walk, I can focus my thoughts to keep trying, keep getting better, and to be at peace with this new me. More than anything, I wanted to be peaceful with my new life. It turns out that it is possible to find peace.

During the early years of recovery, the gauntlet kept appearing at nearly every turn, and I had choices every single day. The secret was in not quitting. Not quitting meant learning to drive again and tying my shoes with my right hand. Not quitting led me back home to kids and dogs. Not quitting took me back to work. Not quitting even eventually got me out dating again. And not quitting helped me see the gifts in loss.

I can no longer wear high heels, but I can walk. I do not often travel on a plane alone, but I can think clearly and speak decisively. I couldn't, and still can't, cut my own steak, but I can cook dinner and open a wine bottle. I can't zip up my dress, but I can put on pantyhose one-handed. And I can view this "me" with compassion and humor. I deserve that much.

Over the years, I've made peace with my cane and now see it as a reason to keep going. The cane means I can do anything or go anywhere. The mechanics of movement may have changed but I have no excuse to stop moving. Although I have accepted the limitations I now have, the potential for greater freedom is something I hope for. My cane is a symbol of me getting where I'm going, and has become a friend.

Occasionally, someone will hold a door for me, and inquisitively look at me. If they ask me what happened, I'll sometimes tell the stroke story. It used to be that I led every conversation with the stroke. Today, all these years later, I lead with other things, things that aren't centered on me. That's the resolution of this whole thing, my ability to accept who I am today and to see others around me.

I know now that my stroke was a gift to help me focus less on the woman in the mirror, pay attention to life as it presents itself, and encourage others in struggle.

Susan Purifoy is the director of Convey Services at Copper Services in Atlanta, Georgia. A stroke survivor, she is devoted to enriching others and encouraging their success. Susan helps business leaders promote and deliver business content to the marketplace, and works with speakers, authors and subject matter experts to increase their visibility and achieve greater success. The mother of two children, she supports the National Stroke Association, and is active in her church and community.

Marcie Mauro

"What else is possible?"

- Access Consciousness

Chapter Twenty-One
STEPPING ON
(AND STAYING ON)
THE PATH

With head in hands, I sense my mood changing. That dismal, all-too-familiar feeling is coming over me again. I get like this when I'm overly tired or on the verge of making an important decision. It's my body's way of letting me know that something needs to shift. I briefly acknowledge that I need to reclaim my sense of self-care if I'm truly serious about being a powerful leader in my work as a coach. If I can't get out of my own head, out of my own way, how will I help other women to do the same? I decide to take a quick break.

I get up from my desk and walk upstairs to grab my glasses. My bed is calling me; I collapse into it and bury my face in a pillow. My heart is racing. My mind is stuck on repeat, playing the old tapes of my inner critic. *You can't do this. Who do you think you are? Haven't you put your family through enough by chasing your dreams? You'll never make it. Just give up now and create financial security by getting a job.* I've heard it all before, in one version or another, for most of my life.

The anxiety builds and my heart continues to pound

so rapidly that I wonder if it will break. In this moment of fear it does feel broken, sad, heavy and, like me, exhausted. I haven't gotten a proper night's sleep in months because I've been burning the candle at both ends with my career. Now the divine spirit within me is like a flame flickering in the darkness, ready to go out.

Can I really make my entrepreneurial dreams come true? I think I can but do I truly believe it? I feel alone. I want to cry. I try but the tears won't come. I keep wishing that this time my life, things will be different. I've been down this road before. Perhaps this time, worry will dissipate and confidence will prevail. I squint my eyes and let out a silent scream in desperation. Then I hear it. Softly echoing through the house from my office downstairs, I hear "the" song, and Bob Marley is singing, "Every little thing's gonna be all right..." I say "the" song because it has serendipitously found me at the most perfect times of need in my life, including this one.

I immediately feel a sense of calm. Relief washes over me and I feel reassured that everything is going to be all right. I may have allowed the hesitant parts of me to dominate just a few minutes earlier, but now I find the courage to negotiate with them. I begin to trust my inner knowing. Yes! It is going to be all right.

I shoot out of bed and grab my sneakers. "I need to walk," I say aloud to proclaim my follow-through. Walking is when I feel most inspired and connected to my Self. It is from the place of Self that I know in my heart I'm meant to be a successful entrepreneur and be a stand for people loving what they do so they can create more peace and prosperity in their lives.

The first few steps as I walk down my long driveway are

the hardest to take, much like the beginnings of creating a business. It's tempting to talk myself into a quick jaunt to the mailbox and back because I have "so much to do" and "don't have time" for a walk. After all, it's far too easy for entrepreneurs - especially solopreneurs - to get caught up in the small steps rather than stay focused on the outcomes and the journey.

A burst of commitment runs through me as I deeply inhale the crisp air; I allow it to fill my lungs with a sense of hope. Inner calm expands within me. I close my eyes for a second; a resounding YES! reverberates through my body once more. I open my eyes and remain focused on the intention of this walk, the intention of this journey. The first thing I see is the familiar big hill that is an inevitable part of my route. *Ugh!* I think. The inner critic returns: *Oh, Marcie, just turn around and go home. You're too physically depleted. Besides, you need to get back to work; remember how much you need to get done? You're taking time away from growing your business. Come on, just go home.*

It's a perfect depiction of my entrepreneurial oscillation between exuding confidence while trusting my intuition and then drowning in self-doubt. I manage to slowly turn down the volume on my inner critic and pick up my pace. Soon I am charging up the hill. I am reminded that taking care of myself is THE best thing I can do for my business, even if it seems like the last thing I have time for.

After a while en route, I invite my inner critic back for a conversation, but this time from a place of curiosity rather than pushing it out of my awareness. I tell this insidious voice of doubt that even though I get frustrated with it sometimes, I know that it has my best interests in mind and is only trying to help me.

"What are you concerned about if I were to lead my life and my business from a place of confidence all the time, rather than from fear and self-doubt?" I ask aloud.

The critic answers: *The more confidence you have, the farther you'll soar and the harder you could fall.*

"Wow," I respond, "I had no idea that you cared so much about me. All this time I thought you were trying to make sure that I failed."

As I start to head back home, my tempo syncopates with flashbacks of times when I had fallen. When I had pursued what I thought was a right decision and it was not. When I gave something my best effort and stumbled nonetheless.

Had I not been walking, it could have easily become swallowed up by negative self-talk again; however, physical movement creates a "detached observer" perspective to these familiar stories. It forms a protective barrier around my heart so that pain and shame can't creep in.

I silently asked myself: *What have I learned through each of these stories? How have I grown?* As each story answered separately, I began to see the growth. I began to see the light. One taught me to pay more attention to my contributions to outcomes rather than wait for things to come together on their own; it's about taking action. Another told me that without this experience I wouldn't have realized how deeply my gifts could impact others. I may have continued to disempower my strengths, not helping as many people as I could. And yet another story told me that it happened the way that it did to support me in embracing my inner guidance and following my heart, even if it meant disappointing others or taking huge risks.

It's interesting that when we take the fear and judgment out of reflection, it creates an opportunity for resolution and clarity. These stories had been haunting me for years, paralyzing me from truly stepping forward as a more powerful leader. The fear of failure kept me stuck in overwhelm, spinning my wheels, not taking care of myself and grasping for threads of success. The funny thing is, the very antidote for overcoming fear and getting into action was to tune in and honor my needs for self-nurturance by taking bits of time away from my business. That's where the alchemy and inspiration began to happen.

> " *I almost didn't realize how deeply my gifts could impact others.* "

And it all started with those first steps. Here's what happens next as the walk continues.

I notice that I'm finally heading back down that first treacherous hill. I have slowed my pace yet I'm soaring, present and awakened. I think to myself that I am surely not alone in this experience. In fact, most (if not all) entrepreneurial women work consistently at balancing their lives while fulfilling multiple roles in each stage of their personal and professional growth. The fear of failing never completely goes away; it will always have the potential to leave us stuck and fatigued. When this happens, we are not able to step out into the world and reach the people we are meant to reach. We are not able to create the impact that we are meant to create.

I have learned that the key to being empowered is to embrace the fear with curiosity and gratitude because it is there to help us, not hinder us. We must acknowledge the gifts in our shortcomings. The only way to do this, in my opinion, is to return home to ourselves, to our internal guidance system, and nourish our minds, our bodies and our spirit. In doing so, we take a stand as entrepreneurs, as women, as leaders.

Fear is not an indication that you should give up or that failure is imminent. It's simply an opportunity to check in to see if you're on track, if you are growing in the work you are meant to, if you are helping the people you are meant to help, if you are caring for yourself in the way that you would care for others. Embrace the fear, for on the other side of it is the success, freedom and fulfillment you seek. It's not about being perfect, or trying to be someone that you're not. Rather, it's about being YOU... the real you. It's about fully showing up, with all of the beautiful imperfections that make you incredible.

As I finally reach the front door after my walk, the air feels warmer, the sun seems brighter. I have renewed clarity that I am on my Path. I am home.

*After more than a decade in the wellness industry and years trying to find her place in the professional world, **Marcie Mauro** realized it was up to her to create a career that works with her family-oriented lifestyle without sacrificing financial success. She is dually certified as a Money, Marketing, & Soul® and Money Breakthrough® coach and enjoys serving clients internationally. Marcie's energy and passion led her to create a business that fuels her spirit, helps the world, and gives her plenty of time to enjoy her boys (her husband and son). Now she's driven to help more women do the same - have more freedom, more fulfillment and more fun creating a satisfying and financially rewarding business they love. Visit www.MarcieMauro.com.*

Henriette Ashi Clark

"The greatest mistake you can make in life is to continually be afraid to make one."

\- Elbert Hubbard

Chapter Twenty-Two

STEP OUT OF YOUR FEAR AND INTO YOUR LIGHT

*A*s the owner of InSight Imaging, an elective 3D/4D ultrasound center, I consider it such a blessing to be able to do what I love, live my passion and celebrate such exquisite times in the lives of my clients - the birth of a baby and, along with it, the birth of a mother, a father, a new family.

If you had asked me if I ever thought I would own a business, the answer would have been a resounding "no." How audacious of me to even think that I could or should run a business. Years ago, fear and self-doubt would have threatened to stop me in my tracks - the same fear and self-doubt felt by most women. Many have asked me, "How did you do it?" This is my story.

I was born in Beirut, Lebanon and came to the United States as an infant. My parents had three children - two sons and a daughter. My mom was a stay-at-home mom and my dad showed us what hard work was all about. My father never missed a day of work. He took pride in all that he did and believed anything less than 100 percent effort was unacceptable. He expected the same from his children and often told us that our efforts and actions not only reflect upon ourselves but, more importantly, they reflect back on him and our mother. They taught us with words and actions about personal responsibility and accountability, and having a strong work ethic. They encouraged us to follow our dreams. My parents loved us equally and made no distinction among the three of us, but I always felt that college and career success was something reserved for my brothers. We were close in age, with me in the middle, two years younger than my older brother and two years older than my younger brother. I was always proud to be their sister, proud of their successes and happy to stand in their light.

After I graduated from high school, it was time to build my life. I had a job working in accounting for a large company – a job that I excelled in. And soon I became a wife. Life looked good from the outside - I had a loving family and wonderful friends, but I was restless. I had always wanted to go to college and be in the medical field, but a little voice in my head always talked me out of it. What if I wasn't smart enough? What if I couldn't handle it? What if I failed? What if I succeeded? This voice lived in me my entire life, and I thought it was there to keep me safe - but as I grew and matured as a woman, another voice that encouraged me to follow my dreams was trying to be heard. So, I decided that I would go to college.

I was fascinated by ultrasound technology and wanted to be a sonographer. I pushed back the fear (which literally felt crippling at times), registered at the university and was accepted into the program. While getting ready for my first day of class, the fear was so palpable that I wanted to quit before I got there. Thankfully, quitting wasn't an option and by the end of my first day,

I was giddy. Though difficult, I loved the coursework. To add a little fun to the mix, I had recently become a mother; my son was born during my first semester. The "former" voice was there every day telling me why I couldn't and shouldn't continue, but I was committed now and would see it through to graduation.

I loved the hospital atmosphere and was hired prior to graduation. Most of my classmates saw this as a huge accomplishment but I watered it down. I'm not supposed to succeed or be in the spotlight. I just thought they were in need of a worker and I happened to be there at the right time. I couldn't give myself credit that I was a good, even excellent, sonographer. I loved working with patients and the more I learned, the more I loved ultrasound. My little negative voice never left me. I kept studying and learning, wanting nothing more than to excel at sonography. In fact, I would say that the fear was instrumental in keeping me learning. Of course, the dreadful day came when I was presenting a case to a radiologist, and a few other doctors were in the room. One of the doctors asked me a question and I just didn't have the answer. I was mortified. I felt as if I had a spotlight shining on me. I stood frozen, heart pounding and feeling flushed. I heard myself say, "I don't know." I waited for the response, the judging, the comments, the ridicule... but there was none. In fact, the doctor told me that he was more afraid of someone who thought they had all the answers and had nothing to learn than by someone who was bold enough to say they didn't know. Me? Bold? No one had ever described me as bold. I should have learned a very important lesson that day: I could survive being in the spotlight, being on the spot, and could handle it. However, the little negative voice justified this as the doctor simply being nice. For the first time, I wanted to fight the negativity inside of me and tell

193

that voice to "SHUT UP!"

While I truly loved my work, my personal life took a few twists and turns. I had two very close calls with death. I was blessed with a beautiful daughter; however, during my pregnancy, I developed bacterial pneumonia and serious pregnancy complications, as well as a seemingly uncontrollable infection. The doctors told my family that they had basically given up hope for me and were trying to save my daughter. My recovery was slow and returning to work in a few weeks was not a reality so I suddenly found myself a stay-at-home mom. I had been working since I was 17 and the break, although unplanned, was a welcome change. I loved being home with my children, made new friends in the neighborhood and settled into my life. Then came another close call when I developed a large blood clot. The size and location were considered non-survivable, but by the grace of God I escaped death a second time. It took nearly a year to clear the clot and another two years before doctors felt that it was safe enough for me to stop daily blood thinners. The clot permanently damaged the veins in my leg. I would be in pain daily, yet I felt grateful.

After a few years I was ready to go back to work, but found that the negative voice was even louder. Fear and uncertainty returned. Where would I work? Who would want someone who had been out of the field for such a long time? Hospital teams are close knit - how would I fit in? I promptly talked myself out of it. The positive, encouraging voice buried under the fear was still there, too. I wanted and needed to do something, to do more, but who was I?

A daughter, a sister, a wife, a mother, but who was I?

Why did I fear so much and what was I more afraid of - failure or success? I believe I was so much more afraid of success because it puts you out there to be questioned, judged and challenged. I was terrified of the attention that success - if I was lucky enough to achieve it - might bring. This powerful quote from Marianne Williamson adequately describes what I was feeling: "Our deepest fear is not that we are inadequate. Our deepest fear is that we are powerful beyond measure. It is our light, not our darkness, that frightens us most. We ask ourselves, 'Who am I to be brilliant, gorgeous, talented, and famous?' Actually, who are you not to be? You are a child of God. Your playing small does not serve the world."

My life took a huge turn with one email. My older brother - who had reached the heights of business success (see me standing in his light) - had just heard about a new business model called elective 3D4D ultrasound. He sent me an email with a link to the article and one sentence: "Why are you not doing this?" The article was intriguing but I was more stunned that my brother - whom I respected so much for his business acumen and even more so for the man he is - had thought I could do this. *What? Really? Hmmm, could I?* I passed the idea by my younger brother - equally successful in his career and life - knowing he would not sugarcoat anything and would tell it to me straight. I more than expected him to tell me to forget about it, that it wasn't for me, that I couldn't handle starting and running a business; but to my surprise, he said, "This is awesome and you are perfect for it. Go for it. " The new 3D4D technology was simply amazing. To me it was like experiencing a miracle every day. To be able to share with parents their first real glimpse of their babies, to actually "see" them before their birth, is truly inspiring and humbling.

Now my voice of doubt and fear was working in overdrive. Who was I to think I could do this? Where would I get the money? This would be an expensive venture. Who would come and use my services? How would I advertise? What if I failed? What if I succeeded? Yet the other voice way deep down said, "Do it. Try it. Step out of your fear. Step into your own light."

I decided to go to the bank to inquire about a loan. I went with nothing but an idea and was shaking as I arrived. Again, to my surprise, they loved the idea, felt it had promise and told me to come back with a business plan. Umm, a business plan? Here comes the voice: *You don't have a business degree. You don't know what you are doing.* I got in the car and literally shouted, "SHUT UP!" Then I drove home, wrote a business plan and went back to the bank three days later. I started to give up on the idea because my little voice was telling me, *Forget it! You won't get the money. Why would they give it to you?* I got a call two days later. Wow! I was approved!

Oh, no. I was approved! At that moment, I made a decision. I would just have to bulldoze my fear and anyone who fed into it. All the naysayers, the well-meaning friends and family members who told me all the reasons why I couldn't and shouldn't, were ignored - even though I was certain that doing so was to my detriment. I started planning my business, and my passion and excitement grew. I designed my logo and was surprised when others liked it but this gave me a little boost of confidence. I named my business, picked my office location and furnishings, set up my bank accounts and more - all the while telling the negative voice to be quiet. My fear was raging. Failure and success were equally terrifying, but I had to take this journey.

Now, seven years later, InSight Imaging is a success. I am so blessed to be living and working my passion. I have been able to travel the country teaching the art of 3D4D ultrasound and have helped other fledgling entrepreneurs start their businesses. I have built a life that enables me to spend time with my children, work in the field I have a passion for, and help families experience and bond with their babies like never before. I have also been able to teach my children the valuable lessons from my childhood: hard work, personal responsibility and accountability, and the importance of fighting through their fears. I have also taught them to ignore their negative voice, that the fear of failure or failure itself is not the worst thing that can happen to you. Not trying, always wondering "What if?" and not giving yourself the credit that you deserve... these are the things that you should fear.

> " *Failure and success were equally terrifying, but I had to take this journey.* "

I know that I am not the only one who has that annoying little voice, but we are all capable of silencing it. What is it that you want to do but your little voice stops you? Starting a business, going to college, beginning a relationship or ending one, learning to ride a horse, sing or play a musical instrument? It doesn't matter what it is you want to achieve, just make the decision to live your life fully and to step into your light.

I would like to say that the negative voice is silent, but every now and again it nags at me to speak but I won't allow it. I have learned to walk out of my fear and to stand in my own light. As Marianne Williamson reminds

us, "We were born to make manifest the glory of God
that is within us. It's not just in some of us; it's in all of us.
And when we let our own light shine, we unconsciously
give other people permission to do the same. As we are
liberated from our own fear, our presence automatically
liberates others."

Henriette Ashi Clark *is a registered diagnostic medical sonographer and owner of InSight Imaging Inc. in Monroeville, Pennsylvania. The "birth" of Insight Imaging was the culmination of combining a passion for sonography, the desire to become an entrepreneur and the love of helping families share in one of life's most amazing and exquisite experiences. A sonographer for nearly 20 years, Henriette has always shared her passion with students of sonography, tutoring to help increase their knowledge and skills by hosting students just exploring their options with job shadowing and, most recently, by teaching the art of 3D4D sonography to ultrasound centers across the country. Living near Pittsburgh, Henriette is the proud mother of a son, Max, and daughter, Maddie. She shares in her son's passion for music and her daughter's passion for horses. Learn more at www.InSight4DImaging.com.*

Doreen Cumberford

*"Though we travel the world over to find the beautiful,
we must carry it with us or we find it not."*
— Ralph Waldo Emerson

Chapter Twenty-Three
LIFE IN THE CAMEL LANE: LESSONS LEARNED IN THE KINGDOM OF SAUDI ARABIA

*A*s I exited the airplane door, took a deep breath and walked down the steps to finally touch terra firma, I mindfully looked around and drank in the exotic atmosphere of Bahrain. Those first few moments in the Middle East remain imprinted on my memory to this day. I remember gazing up to the dark, starry sky and being struck by the position of the moon, which seemed to be lying on its side - not quite upright and definitely not where it normally rests in the western hemisphere that I was accustomed to. It felt like a premonition - simultaneously disturbing and peaceful - of some sort of internal shift to come. When my feet hit the tarmac, it was like walking into a fresh, wide-open future that was yet unwritten.

I ended up in this part of the globe after my husband, John, accepted a position with Saudi Aramco, the world's largest oil company involved in the exploration, development and supply of the world's energy. I remained in this strange and wonderful land for most of the next 15 years. During our time with Aramco, globalization became commonplace, the Internet was launched and the world became more interconnected, and the United States invaded then departed Iraq. Our story seemed to parallel that of a shrinking globe, massive diversity and great opportunities for inter-cultural understanding and faith. Walking down those steps with John, I trusted that the giant leap we had just made was going to be an expansive experience full of opportunity and possibility. I couldn't have known to what extent relocating there would shift my perspective on just about everything. There was no sign that said, "Welcome to the Middle East. Prepare yourself for a life-changing experience."

" We were a multi-national tribe with representatives from around the globe. "

This adventure is certainly not unique to me. Expatriates since the early 1930s have made thousands of similar trips to this same part of the world. Many have, in fact, spent lifetimes, even raising several generations of families and launching their progeny as world citizens from the land called the Kingdom of Saudi Arabia (KSA). Yet for me personally, it was a quantum leap. Nowadays, the idea of taking quantum leaps in life is occasionally discussed, this notion that humans can make great strides of faith, enormous jumps in consciousness and major steps in creating our own reality through our thinking. I doubt that those ideas were on the top of my mind as I slowly reoriented our three-year-old daughter and myself to our new life. This tale is about the amazing adventure that we enjoyed, and how my experiences in Arabia essentially changed my understanding of the world and all its peoples.

While living in Yokohama, Japan, my husband worked for Aramco in project management. I had closed my business and given up my career as an interior designer in California in order to set sail on this journey. The morning after our arrival in Bahrain - which was on this occasion a brief 16-hour layover prior to taking one of the shortest international flights from Bahrain to Dhahran in Saudi Arabia, a distance of only about 50 miles - we enjoyed a long walk along the Cornice where we saw some old piers and "dhows", hand-built fishing and sailing vessels used in the Middle East to locally transport fish and other goods. Today, if we were to take that same walk, it would be on the side of a four-lane highway, at the base of two 53-story twin towers. This area is now Bahrain's most prestigious address and a premier commercial development located on the seashore. Synchronized, colored lighting in these two towers flows from floor to floor in the evenings and can be seen from miles away, signaling that this land is a 21st Century beacon for progress and success.

The following morning we flew from Bahrain to Dhahran International Airport and landed in an old, shabby, disorganized place with lines of expatriates from many countries. Often flights arrive simultaneously from Europe, India, the Philippines and Sri Lanka, thus depositing thousands of migrant workers into the Kingdom - all of whom must have papers inspected and visas checked. An Aramco company representative ushered us into the Kingdom with relative expediency then a colleague drove us up to Ras Tanura, a distant settlement and compound situated on the heels of a huge refinery on the shores of the Arabian Gulf. On our first morning in Ras Tanura, we took another walk along the sea front, as we had in Bahrain. After having previously lived in Yokohama, a dynamic, bustling city of 11 million people, this sleepy settlement of Ras Tanura was quite a shock to the system. This felt more like being in a deserted golf resort with few people and little activity, except for employees of Saudi Aramco. In fact, golf carts were the common mode of transportation.

Our arrival in Ras Tanura was marked by a 20-day spell of rain, almost unheard of in the KSA. *How coincidental,* I thought, as I felt a bit like an anomaly myself. I remember peering out of our house window at the streets, and seeing drains that were unable to cope with the water flowing like a river. In the days to come, I would stare out that same window looking for people and seeing little activity, except for during the morning and evening commute to work and school. I felt like I had been dropped onto an alien planet, and I struggled to make sense of this foreign environment, the culture and its people. It was like living behind a curtain, and doing so was made even more pronounced by our distance from much contact with the outside world.

We arrived on December 1, 1995, a time when television satellites were situated on many of the buildings and houses, despite the fact that several years before a decree had made them illegal. Within a few years we were blessed with Internet access (albeit the slow dialup version) and other technological advances such as the international phone service Vonage and, ultimately, a video calling service that suddenly shrank the world and gave us a solid connection to friends and family in the UK and US.

Within a few weeks after arriving, we started adjusting to the slower pace, and I began to think of it as life in the camel lane. My daughter attended pre-school and I had time on my hands to explore the compound and the activities therein. As I began to venture out, I quickly learned many things about the local culture and customs. Prior to arriving in KSA, for example, all expatriates are required to pledge to be good guests and to honor the local customs - everything from not drinking alcohol to women keeping covered and, of course, no driving on Saudi roads. I distinctly remember walking to the gym wearing what I considered to be relatively tasteful exercise gear that I assumed would mollify the local Saudi population; but when a Saudi Security guard followed me for five blocks in his car, I wasn't sure whether to laugh or be dismayed. Perhaps it was because I was a new face in this small community, or he felt that I needed protection. Whatever the reason, it was one of my first introductions to a differing perspective.

Another aspect of Saudi life that became like the signature tune of our living movie was the call to prayer, which occurred five times every day without fail, as well as Ramadan, when fasting is practiced for an entire month during daylight hours. Upon the first sighting of the moon, Ramadan is announced and the entire Hijra calendar is navigated around it. While Aramco expats were afforded the privilege of practicing their faiths peacefully, this was not a situation that existed anywhere else in the Kingdom. The importation of bibles, crosses and Christmas trees was outlawed and yet somehow magically, "Holiday Trees" could be found throughout the compound or occasionally for sale in the commissary. Because we arrived in December, we anticipated a few Christmas festivities on the compound but were surprised by the amount of parties, caroling and people dressed up as Santa Claus. We had to be vigilant in keeping our daughter, Lynsey, from the front window so she wouldn't see Santas whizzing by in golf carts. That Christmas, she asked for a puppy and friends who were already in the Kingdom arranged to get one. It was personally delivered by a jolly expat dressed as Santa who showed up at seven o'clock on Christmas morning in his golf cart - something that Lynsey says she will never forget. Our Christmas celebrations were an example of a lifestyle that reflected a 1950s way of life, a simpler time. Now having made the adjustment back to the US with all its commercialism, we long for those simple, homemade holidays.

Another interesting aspect of life in the KSA was the bond that formed among the expats. We basically lived on a compound surrounded by gates, fences, security guards and (after 9/11) layers of sophisticated technology. I was constantly in a state of wonder and gratitude for the sense of trust, respect and esteem between the expatriate and Arabic communities. Although the bonds of tribes and families run deep, the alliances formed in our expat community were as potent and powerful as any tribe. In fact, the expatriate community came to reflect many small tribes, divided into groups according to interests. There were dozens of activities and creative pursuits to dive into. We were not just "imports", but more so a multi-national tribe with representatives from around the globe. Dozens of nationalities were represented in the company, and this provided all of us with the opportunity to enjoy intimate cultural diversity. Fathers at work got to know each other, and the mothers did so through social groups, volunteer work and children's school activities. Layers of tradition were woven into the daily fabric of KSA life to support the expat population and nurture our community to thrive and grow.

I learned to respect and trust the deep, abiding sense of destiny and wellness that seemed to permeate the souls

of many of the Arabs that I befriended. For the most part, when I witnessed Saudi women's unveiled faces, what I saw were warm, glowing eyes that gave me a peaceful reassurance that I was actually in the presence of a wonderful energized person who wore some sort of invisibility cloak called an abaya. I was privileged to meet many well-educated Saudis who spoke English and were part of the privileged strata of society. Empathy became a commodity, as most of us came to understand the amazingly rapid history of change and modernization that overtook these desert dwellers.

Although definite cultural divides did exist between the local and expat populations, many positive alliances formed; for example, expat and Saudi girls alike played and learned together in the same Girl Scout troops. Girl Scouts has had a long and thriving history of teaching skills and exploration in the Kingdom. Boy Scouts and Cub Scouts also had an enormous presence and many expat parents spent their time investing time and energy in their children's activities to give them the best experiences possible. Thousands of "Aramco brats" (that is, children born and/or raised in Arabia) had opportunities to develop cultural curiosity about others and see the world through another's point of view. These types of interactions among families lent themselves to developing empathy and smoothing the boundaries of radical social differences that were obvious between the cultures, but which ultimately blended and harmonized to produce a society that was unique in all the world.

* * * *

So, how has my cumulative experience in the Kingdom altered my own perspective? In total, my dreams, hopes

and aspirations for the future have changed radically. The opportunity to visit other countries, listen to many languages and observe the interconnectedness as a human race has been a profound process that has encouraged my own empathy. I seek working towards a world in which we can dissolve a portion of our borders, sit and talk evenly, ask questions and acquaint each other with the deep love we individually have for our respective countries.

In my vision, world cultural curiosity would become the norm rather than the exception. We would all be willing to take our own personal quantum leaps and gladly risk (or sacrifice) our outmoded ideas of how to live. This is not only a wish or desire, but a reality in action as demonstrated by the mini-United Nations already harmonizing and functioning as a society in the desserts of Saudi. Almost everyone I meet who has lived in KSA has enjoyed a similar experience of feeling privileged to have been a part of this grand experiment. Not only were we made deeply welcome, we were considered honored guests and for the most part treated as such. Imagine each of us treating each other as honored guests while on this life's journey.

Can we live up to this ideal? Abayas are not just for covering women in Arabia. I have discerned that those of us in the West have our own coping behaviors - or, "mental abayas" - that we use to create a veil of secrecy, insecurity and the illusion of separation. My vision is for all the tribes and nations of the world to sit and to listen carefully to each other, break bread together, get curious about what's possible and learn from the stories that form these ideas. There are more than seven billion of us, so naturally our perspectives differ, but let's move around the table, travel the world, and become allies.

Let's allow the strange and foreign to become subjects of curiosity.

Much like that moon which seemed to be lying on its side when I stepped onto the tarmac in Bahrain in 1995, I sense that I, too, now lie in a different position in the universe. I am continually reminded to slow down, step into the camel lane, and be fully present in every single moment - not seeking to find anything in the future to fill me up and not seeking to relive the past. It is in this moment that we find the most joy, fulfillment, humility, love, grace and inner peace. The Kingdom taught me this, and so much more. May the collective experiences of all of us who have journeyed to KSA contribute to a new tribe called "difference making in the new world." May we share the aliveness and the welcome that we felt while in that strange, wonderful land, and may it awaken us all to a new perspective on each of our lives can truly reflect a higher calling or possibility. May the camel lane be a highway for this new peaceful coexistence.

Doreen M. Cumberford *is a coach, speaker and trainer at "A Wee Bit O' Brilliance." Doreen is a native of Scotland who has lived internationally for almost 40 years. Her career has spanned several continents and countries. From working in British Diplomatic Service in London and West Africa to top sales professional in interior design in California in the 1980s, Doreen brings a breath of fresh air and a new perspective. She has been a mother, volunteer and executive's wife for the past 20 years in Saudi Arabia. Currently she loves coaching and teaching inspirational principles to empower others in igniting their unique brilliance.*

Amelia Roncone

"We must all suffer one of two things: the pain of discipline or the pain of regret or disappointment."

\- Jim Rohn

Chapter Twenty-Four
DECIDE. COMMIT. SUCCEED.

etermining what to do with our lives and what career paths to aspire to are not decisions that can be taken lightly or without significant contemplation. However, many people face the dilemma of uncertainty and emulate traditional models of success; that is, following what family members have done, choosing conventional professions (lawyer, doctor, accountant, etc.), and going with what is perceived to be safe. I was a student of one such school of thought and have learned, through my experiences and work, that we do not need to be constrained to this paradigm to achieve our higher purpose and meaningful success. Life is evolutionary and one must be, as well, in all facets of life. This characteristic is essential to succeed and thrive, especially in today's fast-paced society. Although I had a reputable, secure position as a nurse, there was that inexorable feeling that something was missing. The sense of fulfillment and happiness I deserved simply wasn't there and it led me to two significant questions that undoubtedly changed the course of my life: "What do I do now? and "Do I have the audacity to reach for greater heights?"

211

My professional journey into the real world began with taking a page from my mother and grandmother. Both were professional nurses and led stable, happy and successful lives, so I followed suit. After graduating high school, I went on to study nursing, while supporting myself by working full time. Looking back on those years, it seemed that I was constantly on the "go" without a second to stop and reflect on how my endeavors were shaping my future. I stayed true to the course nevertheless, graduated, and then landed a respectable job in the "big city" as a registered nurse in the neurovascular intensive care unit at the University of Pittsburgh Medical Center. It all sounded great, but I knew that I was meant for more.

Decide

"The possibilities are numerous once we decide to act and not react." -George Bernard Shaw

Well, I didn't necessarily discover the answer, but I discovered a strong sense of direction when my current friend, soon-to-be lifetime confidant, and business partner presented me with an "opportunity" in the oil and gas industry. The opportunity was completely foreign on many levels; however, I was eager to catch up to the curve. Not only did it come with professional autonomy in which I could grow into the business woman that I envisioned of myself, but also the opportunity of uncapped financial growth. Conventional wisdom suggests sticking with what works and is stable, but I took the road less traveled, and it truly has made all the difference.

My new business partner, a tenured professional in the energy industry, had just sold of his share in a company

212

and wanted to capitalize on his experience and knowledge. It was his ownership in a restaurant that spawned the idea to cater meals to men working long hours on the rigs. I was sold on the idea and with my college restaurant experience and was eager to jump on board. Shortly afterwards, We Serve You catering was born and my passion was ignited. We started the company and became equal business partners. Through my work, I was learning about the energy industry and getting a crash course in business management.

Opportunities exist; they always have and they always will. However, one must have the inner resolve and clarity to recognize them when they're presented, along with the fortitude to follow through. Although I was entering an industry I knew little about, I had the confidence in myself and my abilities to stay committed to the path I'd chosen. Grab opportunity by the horns, I say; if not, someone else is assuredly going to take the rewards. Remember, if you wait for every question to be answered, every obstacle to be removed or the approval of others, you will remain safe and static still longing for that void to be filled. Growth requires change, and change always has an element of risk.

It's the "doers" who learn to mitigate these risks and subsequently reap the benefits. In retrospect, I now realize that it wasn't only about a specific "opportunity" or open corporate position that I was being asked to fill. It was about an opportunity to BELIEVE in myself. I spent countless hours comparing the tangibles, such as my 401k, salary and vacation time, but it was the intangibles that deserved more of my attention: my happiness and true passion to help others. What I didn't fully comprehend then and still work on today is that my inner strength will always be the only compass that

I need. Focusing on my inner strength allowed me to follow my passion and be that much closer to personal fulfillment. When you concentrate on what is truly important, you tend to give it 100 percent and the tangibles that once kept you up at night tend to work themselves out. That opportunity was about finding faith and trust in oneself. From that point forward, my belief was unshakable and my commitment to this new endeavor was absolute.

Commit

"The question isn't who's going to let me; it's who is going to stop me." -Ayn Rand

After attempting to balance both catering and my position at the hospital, I found it increasingly difficult to find enjoyment as an RN. As luck would have it, my newfound business partner in We Serve You was beginning yet another venture and again invited me to participate. We Serve You was a startup company at that juncture, and not quite stable enough to allow me to quit my full-time job. I decided to leave the nursing field for good and join him at Specialty Oilfield Solutions as business development of specialty products, and I haven't looked back. The name of the catering company has since been changed to Amelia's Elegant Catering to form a scalable, consistent brand. It is now a majority owned women's business, providing jobs for approximately two dozen women in Pennsylvania, Ohio and West Virginia. Not only has our growth lead to increased involvement in the energy industry, the business has also expanded into different sectors such as weddings, corporate seminars and networking happy hours.

Sometimes life presents us with opportunities to change our lives in ways we never expected. If anyone would have told me five years ago that I would be managing a major division of a multi-million-dollar oil and gas service company, while growing my very own catering company on the side, I would have thought they were crazy. Taking that leap of faith in myself and choosing to ignore the potential consequence of failure has brought me closer to my happiness. I knew, even with the risks in mind, that I had to act as though failure was impossible. My unshakeable belief in my abilities supplied me with the strength to overcome whatever obstacles came along the way. Most psychologists say it's the anticipation of failure that paralyzes, not the actual failure itself. Understand that facing your fears requires mental fortitude, perseverance and discipline coupled with boundless commitment. Once you've committed to the decision, you'll find yourself taking baby steps at first, but with each step you will make bigger strides, put more distance between you and your old life, and get closer to your new goal. You can't not reach your goal.

When I first joined the energy field as business development manager of specialty products for SOS, and the co-owner of We Serve You, I noticed a significant lack of female presence, a major difference from my previous career as a nurse. Where were they? A report commissioned by the White House Council on Women and Girls, which was created by President Obama, concluded that "the reason for the gender pay gap is because women on average choose to work in less stressful work environments and choose jobs in lower paying industries like education and healthcare." Being ingrained in the industry already, I set out to change this statistic.

The first step was to find a professional female mentor who could provide me with insight that I wasn't able to find anywhere. My quest led me to involvement with a professional networking organization called Young Professionals in Energy. Although I did not ascertain the exact guidance I sought, I found YPE to be a valuable organization and a great medium to inspire others. After stumbling upon other women with similar concerns, I decided to give up my search for a mentor and attempt to become one myself. I had an epiphany: I would form a networking group that provides a comfortable, supportive environment solely to the women of the industry to create a place for exchange of ideas, potential for mentorship, and growth opportunities in this male-dominated industry. Here was my chance to pay it forward and instill in other women the effective methods that I used to overcome the daily internal and external skepticism that always resonates but never dissuades the doer.

Young Professional Women in Energy was thus formed with the sole mission to empower and employ more women in the energy industry. It was time to share with others what I had learned and experienced. Empowerment can express many different qualities: an increased sense of personal control, self-sufficiency and most importantly of all, an expansion of choice. As the organization grew in size and prominence, we saw that the strategies we put into place helped the members not only increase their capacity to choose their decision, but in turn gain greater control in their lives.

Choosing to follow your dreams and make a difference in the world will not always be easy. It will not come without second guesses, unforeseen obstacles, sleepless nights and naysayers. You will unfailingly encounter doubters, haters and skeptics. Forget the naysayers. Cast them out of your life. You have repurposed yourself to live your dream. Keep company with the best, meet new people who excel at what they do, and learn to appreciate and recognize support, but just don't expect it from everybody. After all, you are doing what they only dream about. Let nothing deter you from your ultimate goal. If you take responsibility for yourself and your actions, you will develop a hunger to accomplish your dreams.

> " *Decision is your biggest barrier;*
> *if you risk nothing,*
> *you risk everything.* "

My life is so far from where I started but I've never felt more complete, because through all of this, I finally began to put my own happiness first. What do I want? How do I get it? Who can I help along the way? When you take the time to honestly answer these questions and are given the rare opportunity to "live the answers", the liberating life that you once dreamt of is now yours!

I am constantly evolving, as we all should strive to be, and my choices thus far, though difficult, were not impossible. With discipline and clarity, you can change the course of your life, as it becomes a changing, growing extension of your efforts. Like soil in a garden, it will return what is planted; it does not care what is planted. Plant roses, you'll get back roses. Plant ragweed, you'll get back ragweed. The lessons that I've learned along the way will hopefully offer inspiration to those who read this to set off on their own course of discovery. Regardless of your current circumstance, the next move is always yours to make. You have more options than just the chosen path of your current job or field of study. Remember, it is not about the perfect opportunity or all the stars aligning. It's not about deciding for certain at age 18 or 22 or 45 what you want to do with the rest of your life. It's about constantly bettering yourself, questioning, and challenging the status quo. This continuous self-analysis will keep you on your path toward personal triumph.

Discontent can sometimes be the greatest motivator to change. Webster Dictionary defines discontent as "having a feeling that one has been wronged or thwarted in one's ambitions." Sure, nursing is a rewarding career but it was the notion of my personal stagnation that led me to pursue the path I'm on now. That feeling can primarily be attributed to almost any personal or professional advancement. You will see that once you reach that first peak, there are plenty more to conquer along the way. If you are able to harness these feelings, the passion and the commitment will burst out from within you and color everything that you do. The secret is to think differently, plan differently, act differently and not fear the unknown. We are travelers on this path of life, and the more you are aware of your capabilities and strengths, the better road maps you will create to reach your ultimate destination.

SUCCEED

"It is our duty as men and women to proceed as though limits to our abilities do not exist. We are collaborators in creation. You will be happiest and most productive if you love what you do. So do what you love, and get paid for it." - Pierre Teilhard de Chardin

Your life is not a period; it's a comma. It is up to your discretion how you choose to live it and give it purpose. Do what you feel is best and know that habits and positive thinking have a tremendous impact on your success. Habits start as chains too weak to be felt until one day they become too strong to be broken. You will notice positive thoughts infuse your attitude and every tangent of your life.

Decision is the biggest barrier to making a change; if you risk nothing, you risk everything. Most people think and dream of better lives or sexier jobs or being their own boss, but the courage to make that leap is what separates the dreamers from the doers. You are not a finished product if you choose not to be. The greatest hurdle for someone to utilize his or her full potential is to whole-heartedly believe this notion.

I've been a firm believer that the body manifests what the mind harbors. Your mind is a very specific bio-computer that needs detailed instruction and clearly written goals to make dreams achievable. Have a plan to get what you want, and commit to doing whatever's necessary to get it. Initiate action, seize the moment and consciously excel at everything you do. You must be cognizant of the trap of being an individual who is rooted in their station in life. Remember, it takes just as much toil and effort for a bad life as it does for a good one. Which one do you want to live? Your attitude does not affect the world and the people in it nearly as much as it affects you.

Remember, successful people are not people without problems; they are simply people who have learned to use them to their advantage. Being successful, therefore, is a determination of solving the problems that stand between where you are today and where you want to be. Believe in yourself. Develop the steadfast knowledge and belief that you can and will accomplish your goals. Your faith will be rewarded. To see the forest through the trees can be daunting, but if you take these lessons and proactively begin to change your life, the heights you will reach are limitless. You will take off and soar, with your feet never touching the ground again. The only important thing is that you know what you want. The path to a more meaningful, successful life is before you if you just open your eyes. Decide, commit and succeed.

Amelia Roncone wasn't necessarily envisioning a future of entrepreneurial success while in nursing school. But from these humble beginnings and her well-intentioned efforts she became one of the energy industries youngest female entrepreneurs.

This young pioneer founded the non-profit group, Young Professional Women in Energy. Amelia is passionate about instilling positivity in others. She is also a part of Toastmasters International and plans to give back to her community in 2013 with motivational public speaking about the importance of having a vision.

As Amelia's network continues to grow so does her exposure. She and her efforts have been featured in such media as Pittsburgh Business Times, Maniac Magazine, and many more In 2012 Amelia was named the youngest of Pittsburgh Magazine's "40 Under 40," award.

Dr. Christine McGirr

"Being powerful is like being a lady. If you have to tell people you are, you arent."

- Margaret Thatcher

Chapter Twenty-Five
FORGE AHEAD
ONE STEP AT A TIME

On a sunny brisk March morning, signaling the end of winter in Canada with all things fresh and new to come, my neighbor called to tell me that a policeman was standing at my front door. I suspect that I did not hear the knock because I was busy meticulously guiding fabric through my sewing machine. I was finishing drapes for the grand dining room in my new home, a century old house in an beautiful downtown Toronto neighborhood near the lake. Our new home was surrounded by parks and from my third-floor window, I enjoyed an expansive view of the tops of abundant massive oaks, my personal green carpeted skyline. My husband Vic and I had been together for 10 years and married for four. We had wanted to move to this neighborhood for a long time. A little more of a financial commitment than we could handle, we nonetheless took this massive leap. Like many established Torontonians in this community, we felt that the character of an old house in a settled neighborhood close to city amenities was important to raising a family, although we had no immediate plans.

"Someone's at your door, Chris," my neighbor said that morning. "Thanks!" I responded, and hung up the phone. Just then I heard the intrusive knock and, suddenly, I sensed something was wrong. Maybe my husband had stalled his new car or my dog had escaped again, but why the need for a policeman at my door? I bounced down the stairs, peeked through the glass door and saw a grim looking policeman waiting...

*   *   *   *

When I first met Vic, I had been working for 10 years in pharmaceutical marketing. I was doing very well, and had begun consulting and teaching nonprofits how to use the same marketing techniques that large companies used to help them raise money and awareness for their causes. Vic was very successful in his own right, having been a director of a large advertising firm and now working in corporate Canada. Vic encouraged me to start my own company. A good friend of mine, also in advertising, joined me and together we found a perfect untapped niche that we could fill as direct consumer marketers. She worked in advertising for healthcare and lifestyle brands. Utilizing our cumulative experiences, we created a direct consumer marketing business that filled an important gap in the advertising and marketing arena, providing strategic plans for brand development and product launches.

With our contacts and my husband's support and connections, we were excited to take marketing to new heights. Saving our clients' money and time, we would ensure that their brands were "top of mind." Of course, my husband, always an entrepreneur, was our first client.

He had just purchased the Canadian rights to distribute singer/actor Olivia Newton John's new clothing label "Koala Blue." That was our first launch. He also introduced us to the country's leading computer developer and manufacturer. These two big clients were all that we needed to get in the doors of top companies in this and other key industries. Although Vic helped us to secure our first big clients, our hard work and dedication is what built our reputation. We were soon able to rent offices and hire staff.

Seasoned business professionals understand that the first year you feed a business, the second year you feed each other, and the third year, the business feeds you. This was the mantra that kept us going in the early days and by February of our third year, we were well on our way to the business payback. We'd secured five of North America's leading consumer packaged goods and healthcare companies. Our business was doing better than ever. Our staff had grown to 15 and we'd moved into a fabulous old loft office. We began each week with a Monday morning staff meeting. I liked to arrive early at work, especially on Mondays. It was easy for me to get out of bed and go to work. I was happier than I'd ever been. My marriage was great, my business was flourishing and I had a lot to look forward to.

My business partner surprised me very early one Monday morning, just before our staff meeting. When I saw her face, I knew something was wrong. She announced that she'd had enough of running a business. I sat there, stunned, as she broke into heavy sobs and said that she felt it was far too much work and more that she'd bargained for, and she wanted out immediately. I was stunned. I was shocked. I was devastated. This business was like a marriage to me, and

I had no plans for "separation" or "divorce." We had been working well together and finally, our commitment and hard work were paying off.

She was adamant about leaving, and my only choice was to buy her out. Once that was complete, I had the overwhelming responsibility of consoling the staff, reassuring our clients that things would not change and presenting a continuation strategy for the company. At that time, even I didn't understand part of what I was explaining to my employees, as I had never had to deal with a buy-out and reorganization. To this day, I find her actions confusing and know that she missed a great opportunity. Still, I kept myself together and forged ahead to ensure a flawless transition, even though I didn't have time to look at the big picture. I dealt with whatever came up and took things one day at a time. I did not realize just how resourceful a woman I was and eventually the company began to flourish once again. Through it all, my husband continued to provide support by helping me to develop strategy and work with my team to create a shift that would be seamless to our clients.

*   *   *   *

... I opened the door and the policeman identified himself with his badge. My husband was at his Sunday morning hockey game with his best friend Doug. Behind the policeman I could see Doug's wife, Marcy. I thought that was odd for a split second but dismissed it as a coincidence that she was there at the same time. Without hesitation, Marcy stepped inside and put her arms around me. I gave a confused look to the policeman.

"Your husband has been in an accident," he said, then instructed me to get my coat and come with him. From that moment on, all motion slowed down and conversation became clouded, distant, surreal. As if led by another force, I got in the police cruiser with Marcy but I couldn't bring myself to make eye contact with her. Now completely terrified, I asked the officer if my husband was okay. He was calm and polite but curt. "I'm not certain of his condition but we will be at the hospital soon, ma'am," he said.

Even with Marcy there by my side, the fear was palpable and I could feel myself coming apart. I started to rock back and forth, as if attempting to make the car go faster. Terrible thoughts pervaded my mind. My husband had been playing hockey that morning. Maybe he would be crippled and could never play hockey again. That would be the worst, I thought, as I continued to rock back and forth.

Finally, we arrived at the hospital. The officer led Marcy and me to the front reception desk, where the officer gave my name.

"Take her to the quiet room," I heard a nurse say. Goodness, I thought, if this is an emergency, shouldn't everyone be hurrying? My husband is hurt. Why is everyone being so calm? Maybe they have him stabilized and they're going to bring him to me so I can take him home. Marcy and I sat in the quiet room for what seemed like forever, then the door slowly opened. Two doctors and a nurse entered and quietly sat down. All they said was, "We did everything we could. He had a massive coronary on the ice. The ambulance arrived within three minutes but he was gone."

Gone? My God. Impossible. "No, that can't be," I said. "Don't just sit here. Go back and keep trying. He will be okay." He must be okay. I needed him to be okay. I depended on him to be okay. He was not going to be okay. Just a few months after being stunned by the loss of my business partner, I was overwhelmed by the loss of my husband.

How am I going to do this alone? Run a company, remodel a huge home, maintain the expenses of a business formerly run by two and a home dependent on two incomes? These thoughts ran through my head as I was driven home from the hospital.

Two hours after that knock on my door, I returned home and found my house filled with friends and family. One of my husband's team mates had driven his car home and it was now parked in the driveway. How could the car return home and not him? Was I really just sewing curtains this morning? Our friends Doug and Marcy never left my side. Marcy laid beside me in bed that night and just held my hand. We didn't sleep, nor did we speak a word. There were no words that could begin to make sense of this. The important thing was that I was not alone.

The next day was Monday. It was the first Monday morning that I could ever remember when I wasn't happy to wake up. I crawled out of bed and forced myself to go to work. I did not want to be at home. I thought that the familiar work environment would allow me to take responsibility and be in control. My staff was shocked to see me but that was where I felt safe and in control. As everyone greeted me and expressed their sympathies, I looked at each of their faces. Behind their eyes I could see their concern for not only me, but the future of the company and their jobs. Right then and there, I realized that they were counting on me for their livelihood. In spite of my grief, I knew I couldn't quit. I would have to find the courage to run this company on my own now. With the loss of my partner and my husband, I forged ahead.

> *" It was the first Monday morning that I could ever remember when I wasn't happy to wake up. "*

It was not an easy time, and the following days were filled with bad news on top of more bad news about my personal financial situation: My husband had not completed and signed the life insurance policy on his desk. Our lawyer informed me that we didn't have mortgage insurance. My husband had taken part of our savings to invest on the stock market, and his broker called to tell me that due to a margin call, his investments were depleted. Suddenly, it was obvious that I now had a two-income lifestyle with only one income and no backup plan. Could things get any worse? I guess it's true that "things could always be worse" but at the time, it didn't feel that way. I recalled a quote from Abe Lincoln: "When you are at the end of your rope, tie a knot and hang on." I knew what I had to do. Hang on and work like mad. If I didn't, I could lose everything. I was alone in my business and my life but I was hanging on.

For the second time in a year I learned that I am a strong and resourceful woman. Before his death, I truly believed that Vic was the critical ingredient in my success. He had opened many doors for me, but I soon realized that the success was a result of me, my dedication, hard work and passion. I finally acknowledged that while he helped me start the business, I sustained it.

It's been more than 20 years since that awful Sunday in March. After Vic's death, I forged on. I persevered. Some would say that I progressed or even blossomed. With profit sharing I created a dedicated team and together we built a thriving brand and successful business. Many of my employees went on to open companies of their own and some of us remain close to this day. I went back to college and earned two graduate degrees. I finished those drapes for the dining room, finished the remodel and lived happily in the house for many years. My personal business has evolved and now I help entrepreneurs to develop success strategies for their own businesses. I use all the important business lessons that I learned to help others forge ahead when they encounter personal and professional challenges.

When Vic died, the thought of remarrying never crossed my mind. I immersed myself in work and did not think about my personal life at all. My dreams of filling our happy home with children were over. I did not know this then, but my dream of a happy home filled with children was to come true. I remarried and remain married to this day to Mike, my life partner and kindred soul. We fell in love instantly and today, 20 years later, my home is filled with a loving husband, three thriving boys, two successful careers, some politics and civic duties, writing and lots of love.

When Vic died, I thought my happy life was over. If something sad happens to you, when you encounter a difficult challenge, remember this: Your life isn't over. Just like me, you are strong, capable and empowered. You don't know the resources and power that you can draw from within, especially when you face adversity. Drag yourself out of bed, forge ahead and never underestimate your capabilities.

Christine McGirr, MBA, PhD is the founder of the McGirr Institute, an organization dedicated to fostering the growth and development of entrepreneurial ventures. A business analyst, author, speaker and certified executive coach, Christine has led strategic business development plans for a broad spectrum of multinational packaged goods companies elevating major brands to top ten status, resulting in significant corporate growth and profitability. Her passion is to work with women entrepreneurs to launch their business, develop new ideas and keep them inspired. She and her husband Michael have three grown sons and live in Toronto, Ontario, Canada. Learn more at www.ChristineMcGirr.com.

"Nobody can go back and start a new beginning, but anyone can start today and make a new ending."

- Maria Robinson

Here's to Your Empowered Life!

Made in the USA
Charleston, SC
11 April 2013